Trauma Bonding

How to stop feeling stuck, overcome heartache, anxiety and PTSD – Includes Q&A and case studies

Dr. Annely Alexander

Table of Contents

Introduction

S he appears at a family gathering with heavy make-up that fails to disguise what looks like a black eye. He doesn't attend. You take her aside and ask, "What's the matter? Don't tell me he's hit you again!" She brushes it off and walks away.

Later on she says to you in a whisper, "Please... Don't worry about me. We're all right: he's having a bad time at work recently, that's all. Yes, we've had some arguments, but it's OK. I can handle it... I know you and he don't get on, but you have to understand that I still love him."

Do you know someone like this? Or, do you think you might BE that person?

What about this case? She's horribly rude to him, even right in front of his friends and family. It's clear that she totally resents the way he loves their children. She's gone through their money at an alarming rate, but just how much she's spending is becoming difficult to know because he's stopped talking to you about it, even though you're his childhood friend. You've been critical of her, and he just becomes defensive.

Now you've just heard that he's gone and bought her a second engagement ring. Why? Was the first one not good enough? Once again you find yourself challenging your old friend. He says, "You don't understand. That woman has the ability to make me feel like a hero. She's an artist with an artist's temperament, and when she's flying she can take you with her! She can make me feel loved the way I never knew when I was growing up..." You just roll your eyes.

So, do you know someone like that? Or can you see yourself in that description?

Maybe this situation is like one you've seen before. Sadie's worked for ten years in her job. A small family firm. She has to do just about everything in their catering business, from the cooking to the book-work, even sometimes driving the van. She's earning a pitiful wage, even though she's almost never off sick, and works longer than any of the family do. If anything goes wrong it's always Sadie's fault, according to them, though you're more interested in their getting the orders right, than in hearing excuses.

You feel sorry for Sadie, and one day when you get the chance you ask her why she doesn't get another job. She says it would be too much of a strain to change; you point out that she has an awful lot of strain already. Then she says: "I couldn't do that to them, just leave. I mean, they've given me a job all these years. I'm so thankful to them..."

What about that situation?

The common factor is that all these people are victims: they're being hurt and used, to the point that they're suffering from TRAUMA. Yet they all maintain, sometimes with considerable anger toward anyone who wants to point this out, that their abusers love them, or are generous, kind, and patient. Sometimes they'll insist they themselves are at fault, not really worthy of laying a complaint. You become angry when you hear this, and battle to understand what's going on. There seems to be an odd kind of BOND between abuser and victim.

You might just be the person you've been reading about! You also find that you can't understand why you react as you do, nor can you accept the criticism of other people who seem to judge you. Yet deep down, you know that you need help.

That's what this book was written to do. We explain what TRAUMA BONDING is: why victims sometimes become deeply attached to their abusers in love-relationships, families, work-environments, social clubs, or even what should be friendship... and think, feel, hope and insist - quite wrongly - that the one who hurts them actually loves them! Then we will show you how to recognize and understand trauma bonding; and lastly, most importantly, how to free yourself.

Give yourself some time to read this book. Relax, be calm: we're here to help.

Chapter 1
What is Trauma Bonding?

T o start with, ask yourself this very important question: "If I had a good friend who had a relationship like mine is, would I tell that person to get out of it? Would I feel sympathy for them, maybe say that I'd understand just exactly how they felt?"

Yet you are in such a relationship yourself! Or if you know someone you think might be, do you hear them giving advice and sympathy, with feeling and compassion, to other people in toxic relationships - and wonder to yourself why they can't take their own advice? Perhaps it's because they are trapped: it's trauma bonding...

To explain these words: someone who is a victim forms an attachment or sympathy to another person who is hurting them in any way, or denying them freedom. The famous "Stockholm Syndrome", where hostages were held in a bank by terrorists, and during their captivity somehow began to admire, feel for and almost love their captors, is a similar phenomenon, though in some ways it is different. Enough that it demonstrates a human survival-strategy that looks to be the opposite of what you might expect in such a situation.

Trauma bonding usually happens with an abuser who is a narcissistic personality. Narcissism comes from the Greek legend of Narcissus, a hunter who was so good-looking and proud that he despised those who loved him, prompting some of his would-be lovers to commit suicide to show their devotion to him! The gods punished him by making him fall in love with his own beautiful reflection in the still waters of a spring; and he pined away in despair... In other words, narcissists are self-obsessed, proud, and love only themselves.

In unhealthy relationships one can find intense attachment even when one partner puts down and devalues the other; says one thing in one moment and the opposite in the next; treats the other as a thing instead of a human being; denies the truth or accuracy of the other's views, and there is just generally a sense of chaos, confusion and restlessness. There will be cycles of cruel behavior followed by brief "sunny" periods, and from outside you can see that the victim is completely confusing cruelty with love.

What kind of cycles might you see in a traumatic relationship? It begins with putting the abuser on a pedestal and thinking that everything is ideal, then follow stages of being devalued and rubbished, then the victim is emotionally thrown away, and lastly he or she tries to pick up the pieces, reconcile with the narcissist... and then it starts all over again. There is something very like addiction here, whether it be to drugs, sex, foods or gambling. The words "Trauma Bonding" were first used to describe addiction to types of sex-behavior, actually. A healthy relationship is quite different: if a healthy relationship ends, whether by mutual agreement, circumstances, or even death, there will always be a sense of gratitude. This isn't to say there will be no pain: but rather that you will know within yourself, and be able to say, that you are a better person as a result of having had that bond with a significant other.

It is important to look back at the fact that healthy relationships can end. The emotions of two people who feel attracted to one another can eventually start changing as they realize they're not actually compatible. This realization can hurt, but it heals! Psychologists remind us that traumatic, dependent relationships, when they end, manifest such intense, gnawing grief that on closer inspection it's seen to be very different from feeling thankfulness, or having loads and loads of happy memories. The traumatized victim is literally shouting, "I can't live without you! How dare you go away? I gotta have you!" He or she is actually going 'cold turkey' as the enslaving drug suddenly runs out.

There's something like gambling addiction here. Why does old Mr. Jones spend most of his money on buying lottery tickets? "Because," he might say, "I want to win the jackpot. It's one million dollars!!" Week after week as he fritters away his hard-earned pension money, he keeps on trying, believing that perseverance will win him the whole sweepstakes. Most of the time he gets the news that nothing's been won.

Occasionally he does win - a few dollars. This spurs him on frantically to gamble more, blind to the fact that the vast majority of people playing the game will never win the jackpot, and blind to the fact that he's owing money on the flat he rents! In a similar way, a trauma-bonded man in a toxic marriage might keep on and on giving love, attention and money to a parasitical spouse. He almost cries with joy when she warms up and responds with kind words, which she can do on occasion; but this just isn't happening very often. Yet he insists that it proves he can win her constant love and affection, if only he tries again... as if that made up, anyway, for her constant demands for what she wants, and the fact that she has spent a fortune!

Childhood is a very important time, and we all learn about bonding in our early years. Often the experiences are mixed, and some children are soon exposed to a cycle of rejection, changing moods, denigration, manipulative displays of what a parent makes to look like love, and so on: the toxic cycle seen in adult traumatic-bonded relationships. Our 'inner child' who wants love desperately soon recognizes something in adulthood, that looks like a parent's 'saccharine love', and now grown-up, he or she also re-lives the cocktail of defensive strategies and emotions used early in life, when forming a relationship that is becoming traumatic. This rapid up-welling of really powerful emotions from our most vulnerable and dependent years is just that, rapid! What can happen is that somehow it's all so FAMILIAR, we fail to see that it isn't new, and isn't based on real knowledge of someone else. If it's so powerful, it can also feel a lot like falling in love. Even though it isn't real love!

Very little kids can't divorce their parents or shop around for other options. They have to survive. Their primary caregivers are the ones who teach them right from wrong; alas, for some of them it's a jungle in there, never mind out there! Might is right in that jungle, and what an abusive parent says and does must, supposedly, be right even when it's violent, selfish or chaotically inconsistent. This means that, for example, a child will learn that lying to get things out of people, justifying her parents' actions even when she knows of no reason for such behavior, hiding her failures from them so as to keep her peace with them, even hiding their malice towards her grandparents, is what you have to do to get on in life. She's easy to blame, and so she learns to accept false accusations. Anything rather than face the volcanic explosion that results if she tries to stand up to them, when she's blamed by mistake. All of this can be 'un-learned' only with effort and the help of good people, and sadly, that isn't always available. It will carry through to her teen-age and adult life.

As you read through this introduction, it's probably a good moment to make a very important point. Being abused emotionally as a child is not the same thing as saying someone was abused sexually. Many children or teenagers are badly and cruelly treated, and it's all by words and maybe omissions. That does NOT make abuse acceptable: to say, "Sticks and stones may break my bones, but funny words don't hurt" is actually not true, and most of us know it.

What about children and young people who are forced to take part in sexual activities with adults, or enticed into them without being able to understand that this is wrong for anyone of their age? We care very much about helping you, if that is what happened to you. Yes, that is the deepest abuse and cruelty, and it is also emotional abuse as well, of a very intense kind. This also speaks to those who have been sexually-abused in an adult relationship. Everything that is written to help people become free of trauma bonding in any relationship, past or present, will be relevant to you. Anybody who is trapped in an abusive relationship or who was in one, needs the help of other people to be healed. This is a fact of being human. We can't do a D.I.Y. job on all our relationships; we're social animals, healing and growing in a world of other humans. Listen carefully and understand that IT'S NOT YOUR FAULT. More will be explained later. You'll need to seek help, as will others; but now, be calm and carry on reading. For everyone reading this, the following chapters of the book will explain things in more detail and help to sort out what may seem to be some very new ideas and concepts, or confusing details.

If you know someone who has definitely been emotionally traumatized as a child by, for example, a parent with a narcissistic personality, then you know that he or she has been a victim. However, it is unjust to assume that the abuse was sexual. If it were, it's likely to be very well-hidden by both victim and perpetrator. In no way is this said so as to ignore sexual abuse. Yet you can try first to understand psychological suffering and the way its victims behave, because a victim will need your understanding, as well as to understand himself or herself.

Some more vocabulary: you might be familiar with the word, 'sociopath', in which case bear with us. For those who don't know, a sociopath is an otherwise mentally-intelligent, physically-healthy individual whose social interactions are, however, warped. He or she sees other people merely as things to be used. That doesn't mean the sociopath can't understand them. Yes, there always seem to be some really significant little details they fail totally at understanding, but most sociopaths can be surprisingly good at seeing what is going on in other people's lives. They suffer from no illusions caused by the desire to be kind! In their inmost parts is a monstrous pride, and no-one, but no-one is thought to be loving enough towards them, or sufficiently understanding, or kind enough. Many people are clumsy in human emotional understanding; that is NOT sociopathy. The word 'psychopath' is often used in the same way, and it shouldn't be. A psychopath is better thought of as someone who has a mental illness such that he or she cannot judge reality properly. It isn't caused by ill-will, and this poor individual, occasionally dangerous because of being unable to understand what is happening around him or her, is far more likely to be attacked or mistreated by others. Such people may not be able to defend themselves at all. The sociopath spends every waking moment defending his or her interests, by contrast!! Though this is an over-simplification, it is helpful to think of the psychopath as the woman who thinks she's Cleopatra reincarnated, and sits regally in her chair in the asylum, ordering the nurses about as if they are servants, asking for asses' milk for her to take a bath in! The sociopath is the murderer in the 'whodunit' novel who bumps his father off on a dark night during a family gathering, because his miserly Dad wouldn't pay for him to go to an 'Ivy-League' Law School... Narcissists are a type of sociopath, perhaps one of the more easily-recognized kinds, being totally 'in love' with themselves, as explained.

A feature of narcissists is their ability to draw others' attention and to be utterly charming. Like a Venus Flytrap plant, the trap works because the plant is attractive, and because the entrapment is highly effective! Gifts and fine words flow, promises are made, and beautiful stories are told about what the future will be in love... or in business. (There's not much difference to a narcissist!) Yet all of these things do not reveal what a real, inner, day-to-day person is like. It's all truly confusing when the hard, cruel reality of living with the narcissistic sociopath sets in; a violent contrast.

In such circumstances, both victim and abuser seem to behave irrationally. Victims find their desire to justify the lover they've bonded to makes them say stranger and stranger things; those who can admit that their relationship was unhealthy are still insistent that they miss the one who's dumped them to date someone else, for example. They'll say it's hard to live with the abuser, but that it's just as hard to live without that person... Their deep, unmet childhood needs cause such pain, as we have explained, when the comfortable, familiar discomfort they grew up with (and drifted back into when they met the narcissist) is torn away from them once more.

This is why it will be a struggle to leave a trauma-bonded relationship, maybe even at first harder than to leave a normal one. If that's your case, don't lose heart - once you start to understand what's been happening to you, you will feel better, and more encouraged to make the effort later on.

Anyone who is in a toxic, dependent business or other relationship will also need to consider these things mentioned thus far. In business, as with family and sexual ties, some people will be in a serious money-crisis if they were to leave their abusers. We do not ignore or belittle this. What can be said is that the mental strength to plan one's future life and to attain financial freedom is part of becoming emotionally free, and that those two freedoms will go hand-in-hand. You to need to find psychological help!

The road to healing and recovery, which will have much more light shed on it in the following chapters, is going to involve some important milestones. The first will be ADMITTING THAT YOU ARE A VICTIM OF ABUSE. That would seem a bit shocking to some, even though they might have been quick to admit they'd been having problems. The truth is that their abusers have mistreated them, quite simply, and done what is utterly wicked, to use an old-fashioned word. The second is TO ADMIT THAT YOU NEED HELP, especially to overcome your deep inner hurts from childhood that - for no fault of your own - make you still needy, passive, and feeling helplessly guilty. Another thing to do is to LOOK AT YOUR LIFE IN THE PRESENT. We spoke about the charming promises Mr. Smooth-Operator makes about your future together; we've also mentioned the way in which Ms. I-Want-Your-Money-Honey makes you feel all nostalgic about the time you had together, the whirl of past emotions, after she's whirled off and left you. You need to be aware of what you have - or don't have - in the here and now. Is it worth it? Fourthly, you need to REALIZE THAT THE ABUSE ISN'T GOING TO GO AWAY BY ITSELF. The vicious circle is going to keep turning in most cases. Even if the abuser broke off a relationship or died, that damage would still be there inside you. Part of walking away from these kinds of relationship is to break the chains inside. You cannot assume that your sociopath is going to change: it's not only unlikely, but in your state, bonded to him or her in your pain, you are in no position to influence.

Trying to be objective will have you being factual and honest with yourself about what wrong has actually been done to you. You may be surprised at the number of things you can prove. Yes, everyone does something wrong sometimes... but this will probably begin to look like a run of heartlessness and a tissue of lies, lies and more lies. Sociopaths are liars; and narcissists, pretty good liars, no doubt pretty-looking in a good mood - but lies aren't pretty, they're ugly. They're lies, after all.

Chapter 2
Am I Being Trauma-Bonded? Four Ways to Know

W e have just seen that trauma bonding happens deep inside the human person, where all sorts of hurts and needs from our childhood and our most formative years may be hiding. Not only this, but the chaos and confusion of any broken or dysfunctional relationship will make clear, rational and loving thinking quite a challenge in the middle of all the 'flak'. If you add a narcissist to all that, his or her deliberate deception, lies, strategies and 'mind-games' aimed at causing confusion, are a recipe for a gigantic muddle. There is no wonder, then, that victims will find it very difficult to see exactly what is happening to them and why, even though they can feel it painfully.

This chapter will explain four different ways for people to know if they have trauma-bonded with a significant other.

Having mentioned narcissistic sociopaths again, we need to mention quickly that not all trauma-bonded relationships involve them. The other party may be a man or woman with quite serious faults of character and behavior, but that doesn't make him or her a sociopath! Maybe that other person is a fellow-victim of the kinds of experiences you had in your life, so that you sympathize. That sympathy can sometimes end up as a wallowing-together in the swamp you both fell into! Such love or friendship could change to become something insecure, nervous, even violent.

What everyone who is looking to understand trauma bonding needs to see is that it's a personal problem inside each victim. Each victim, whether the other half of a play starring a villain and a hero/heroine, or a story of two suffering pilgrims on the road of life, has to find healing and break free within... to break free from traumatic bonding. Nevertheless, something in victims of traumatic childhoods tends to draw them to narcissists, like flies to a sticky-paper... the very familiarity of

14

the feelings sociopaths create, as mentioned. Narcissists also, from their side, find traumatized people highly desirable/necessary/useful, and are attracted to them, and often have an uncanny skill in finding their potential victims. So in this book there will also be extensive mention of Narcissists and how to identify them. Just keep in mind that there are common features to all victims who form these unhealthy bonds.

THE FIRST SIGN: MAKING EXCUSES FOR VERY BAD BEHAVIOR

If you find yourself always excusing someone's bad behavior in a relationship, always looking to explain it or minimize it, you might be trapped in a trauma bond. If you suffer extreme verbal aggression, or you're threatened physically, or harmed physically - yet still try to make light of it - how much more likely! It doesn't have to be so serious, though. If you're neglected, treated unkindly, have love withheld from you, that's still bad. Yet you want to help... perhaps you feel that the unhappy childhood of your significant other is reason enough to brush off what he gets up to. Do you feel that you have a duty to make up to her for all she went through in her life, that she's told you about in technicolor? Under a victim's concern for the abuser is a terrible fear of being without someone who needs you, of being lonely and lost. You might be making excuses not so much to explain to yourself why he's unfaithful, but because you feel dependent on him, that you just can't survive financially or emotionally without him. Panicking thoughts victims hear could sound something like these: "I'll never find someone like him again"; "I just have to make this work"; "I can't start all over again at my age" and so on. Victims mistreated by their family might think, "But you can have only one family. Who else would care about me?" So if your emotions keep telling you to make the most of it, while your reason shows you that your relationship's in a crisis, this is a clear sign that you are trauma-bonded.

THE SECOND SIGN: THE MORE ABUSE YOU GET, THE CLOSER YOU TRY TO GET

It's shocking, once you realize it, but people can end up trying to move closer to their abuser immediately after even the most terrible words or deeds. This could be by apologizing frantically, promising to change, or giving in to their demands. Victims can find themselves trying harder and harder to make peace, saying to themselves that peace is peace at any price. They don't rush off to a safe corner to try to lick their wounds; instead, it is as if they beg the aggressor who inflicted the wounds to help them, and put a bandage on those very wounds! Do you recognize yourself here? Or the person you are reading this to try to understand? Trauma-bonded victims can cry and beg for mercy, plead with their aggressors, and offer to take all the blame. They might be doing this because they are terrified of losing that other person they call their loved one. Previous agreements made with them, boundaries set - "It's OK as long as you never see that other woman again" - or the things abusers themselves promised to do, are bent, ignored, all out of fear of the situation growing worse, of losing that other person.

The cycle of abuse may cause someone who is able to stay somewhat distant from their abuser, at times, to move closer just when the abuse is at its peak. Then once again the victim gets some little scraps of love in the first phase, and stays close until she starts being ignored again, snapped at, and so in the next phase she draws back a bit, and the cycle grinds on. Meanwhile, in the minds of the abused, their terror of losing that lover, friend or family-member drives them on, though deep down they are beginning to see that it's NOT going to get better.

THE THIRD SIGN: YOU THINK YOU'LL DIE WITHOUT THEM IN YOUR LIFE

It's been said just now: you think life will never be the same again without your abusive partner. She's giving you everything that makes life worth living! Life without her would be a dirty, grey desert... How much more is it a sign of trauma bonding when the abuser has dumped the victim already, or the victim has had to flee to safety to protect herself physically, yet there is a feeling of missing them, shock and grief at being away from them! But we must not blame victims. Everyone has to understand that there is a terrible, mental addiction here. Researchers have discovered that the same chemicals made in the brains of drug-addicts, are those in the brains of the trauma-bonded! We mentioned the fact that trauma-bonding was first described in the setting of sexual addiction. It is hard to get off addictive drugs, and some say harder to get off addiction to a person - but once more, don't despair. It's possible and it happens. To stop taking the drugs is to get back to where you were; to be free of a trauma-bond is to grow as a man or a woman, in a way you hadn't ever before. The prize is even greater, and in both cases it brings peace.

If you feel guilty about leaving your abuser, indebted to him or her, or just depressed about losing what feels as if it has so much promise, understand that these are not logical, and they're NOT true feelings of love: they are horrible side-effects of the chemical warfare that's been going on in your brain, to put it that way. It sounds shocking, but take it kindly: it means, don't feel guilty; you're not indebted; and you won't have to feel depressed!

When victims understand this, it sheds light on why they feel trapped, and explains why they can't stop loving (as they see it) the abuser. It explains why the cycle of bad treatment keeps on turning, why as much as part of them DESPERATELY wants to shake it off like water from a duck's back, to walk out of an abusive situation, it seems that they just cannot get around to doing so; that there's some good in it they just HAVE to cling to. They are indeed trauma-bonded.

THE FOURTH SIGN: YOU WANT TO JUMP FOR JOY WHEN THEY ACTUALLY DO SOMETHING GOOD

Do you suffer, and suffer, and suffer, and then Mr. Stormcloud suddenly smiles a sunny smile at you, or tells a funny joke? And then you experience a rush of relief. You start to hope that things are going to get better. Maybe Mrs. Shrillchafe stops her machine-gun of criticisms of you and tells you what happened when there was a car-accident in the street, that she witnessed... a normal conversation for a change. You sigh with happiness and enjoy the relief of a non-stressful communication, in fact you want to jump for joy - maybe it's a sign! Yeah, it's a sign; but not what you think. Or maybe the strong emotion (the following is important) could be on the part of your otherwise abuser: he or she could, for example, break down and cry about the affairs they've had. A man might even say that he needs counseling; say, on bended knee, that he wants you to forgive him. It makes you feel almost excited... what if?

You feelings are the first symptoms of the drug you're hooked on, psychologists tell us. They are so quick, so one-quick-fix actually. All seems to be rosy again, and the memory of being mistreated, some shocking deed to you or to someone else, becomes dim. Even when it was only... yesterday? This is a sure sign of trauma bonding.

Look at it: what you just got is no more than most people get on most days. If you get kindness or even just relief once in a blue moon, how is that normal? And the person who gave you a tit-bit of goodness is the very same person who's sucking out so much of your goodness! They're selfish, and they are probably just in the mood for a good chat, which anyone can be. Can't you see that the rapid change in their behavior (e.g. sneered at you this morning, talked about the weather this evening) requires you to forget what only just happened? It makes no sense. They don't make sense. And you, a trauma-addict if that's what you are, are feeling feelings that make no sense.

Chapter 3
Are You in Love or Are You in Trauma?

T he word 'bonding' might seem to be negative when you see it used together with the word 'trauma'. This is not so at all: to use the words, "I love so-and-so" is to say that you have a bond with him or her. If you aren't linked to someone, joined, bonded, then you cannot know them, be influenced by them or influence them: in a word, you can't love them. There are perfectly normal, healthy bonds which everyone alive needs to function as a healthy human and social being.

Good things can and do go wrong, and this is what happens to the bonding process of people who form trauma bonds. Sometimes the words 'trauma bonding' are rendered as 'trauma coupling' instead, to distinguish the good from the bad types of dependency and relationship.

It is quite possible for people to form trauma bonds of different kinds in their different individual relationships, because, as has been pointed out, they are caused to form by deep inner hurts that will affect all of a person's life. They are not restricted to romantic relationships, as we made clear earlier, and can co-exist in that type of relationship and also at the same time be in family ties, for example.

So: what's the difference between a trauma-coupling and a healthy bond?

A trauma-coupling springs out of an emotional, almost physical addiction, as we established. The powerful feelings of relationship-addict are not just 'highs', but 'lows' also, as with any addiction! These emotions will all be familiar from childhood, be they fear, worry, bursts of bad temper, rushes of pleasure and excitement, dreams of future happiness, and so on. One partner might be trying to pull away from the other's intensity, the other trying to push himself or herself closer. There is instability and sudden change in the way that the relationship is maintained: it could mean that someone is impulsive and says things without warning, or makes snap decisions. The word 'chaos' keeps showing up... boundaries that people set because they respect and keep our identities intact, will either not be set up, or will keep on being trespassed. This doesn't mean that there's no pattern of abuse: it's the fact of not being able to predict, for example, that an abuser might suddenly try to do or say something unpleasant that he or she has never done before, just to try it. Trust cannot exist in this poisoned atmosphere... Sometimes it's unclear who exactly is the angry or the insulted one, when the victim of such a bond tries to identify unhealthily with their partner to the point of feeling their emotions FOR them! It is sympathy rather than empathy. In contrast, that might turn into a phase when the angry feelings of one suddenly stop resonating with the other, who tries hard to feel peaceful instead... As powerful as traumatic emotional bonding is, there is a palpable difference in the range of emotions that play out in it, compared to normal relationships: the powerful emotions can be rather limited. For example: a man's anger and his alternating fear are his dominant feelings in his relationship. His other emotions will seem to be hidden. Actually, even his strong feelings of anger and fear look rather stereotypical - always the same issues, the same words, and the same kind of anger and fear. Indeed, people in traumatic bonds hide a lot of their inner personal life precisely because of their intense fears. They simply are not being themselves, but actors on the relationship-stage instead!

A healthy link or bonding with another person is different. Often it is slow and steady in forming, maturing like a good wine... You might object, and point to a 'whirlwind romance' that blossomed into a lifelong marriage as being an exception, but that wouldn't be the case. Even such a relationship was more than the initial attraction. It obviously didn't stop there, but carried on growing and deepening once the two spouses were over their honeymoon. They kept on living and working on their bond in their present tense; and didn't become trapped, looking back to the past at the memory of their first love. Even when it formed quickly at first, it was still peaceful inwardly. Trauma-bonded people are, whether suffering, abusing and being abused, whether drunk with excitement at their idealized first stage, or enjoying the relief such as when Mr. Miser actually felt like giving his girlfriend ten whole Euros and actually did so... all lacking inner peace.

People who trust one another can be authentic. 'Authentic' implies being able to let someone see me, warts and all. A true friend is one whom you can be yourself with. To be like this is to be potentially vulnerable; but where there exists a bond of trust, friends can allow their imperfections, unfulfilled goals, and so on, to be seen - without fear of ridicule, interference or rejection. Boundaries in these relationships are made and respected. Is is understood on both sides what belongs to one friend, and what is in contrast shared by both. Those boundaries make a friendship predictable in a pleasant, un-boring way: each friend knows what to expect and can count on it. In a marriage or other romantic relationship, boundaries could be defined, for example, making space for each spouse to go and spend time with his or her own family. The spouses know they don't have to be together in every waking moment; and they respect the demands those family members make of their beloved other, knowing that a certain amount of time has been agreed on to give them, but which will not be excessive. Their family-members also know that they are not going to be left out in the cold, that the two spouses are not going to shut them out of their life together and social lives.

These are the clear differences. Where, then, does good bonding come from? It's a learned pattern of behavior, learned from parents and anyone who cares for us when we are babies and small children. It's all about receiving love. It's what we need to see from day one! Sadly, no-one is perfect, nor is their care. Childcare that's defective and lacking scars individuals deep within themselves, so that it becomes a life-long task to undo the damage and grow into a balanced and secure maturity. The main areas where children experience problems related to later trauma bonding are as follows...

Conflicted care is when a child is taught that love is conditional and co-exists with neglect. Susie has to impress or charm her parents to get their love. If she fails in their eyes, they grow cold and withhold attention from her. So sometimes she gets it, sometimes not. It's all the more poignant and ironic that any cruelty she suffers is coming from the people who give her more than anyone else. After all, yes, they do give her her meals, her clothes, the roof over her head - and a sword hanging over her head! Susie will be tossed about between the opposites, even though she can probably predict what her parents are going to do, because of the inherent conflict of her parents being both nurturing and yet uncaring.

Unpredictable care happens when a child is at the mercy of an adult's impulses and instability. Not only might little Mike be seriously abused on one day by his mother, but she may just give him gifts on the next; he has no way of knowing what he'll get, or when. It's not just enough to make him afraid of the future or confused, but his mother is robbing him of a very important, primal control over his life. You see, if Mike knew what she wanted of him, what motivated her to reward or punish him, he could try to do what she wanted. If he can't predict her behavior, he cannot control what he will get from her. Pleasing her gets him approval sometimes - but at other times it's useless. It's out of his hands. He's not safe.

Withdrawn or distant care comes from caregivers who may be present physically, perhaps providing meals and clothes, even gifts, but who don't interact enough with a child emotionally. They don't give of themselves. Absent parents are the cause of many problems, as we understand more easily; the father who supplies money to a household from a distance and visits a few times a year is an example. However, the pattern seen in trauma bonding appears to be more of the first type of distant care. It could happen when a parent rejects one child in favor of his or her sibling: the parent is still a parent to the rejected child, and is still there in the home; but he or she has withdrawn affection, has distanced from them.

The patterns of conflicted, unpredictable or withdrawn care do their damage, and the child grows older. The damage will shape and warp all his or her relationships with other people, especially if it's serious, and all the emotions that went with childhood can surface rapidly when he or she meets someone and enters into any kind of relationship that requires a personal bond. Perhaps the new person in his or her life is a repetition, or recapitulation, we could say, of a parent-figure. Let us return to the example of Mike. Now a man, he may meet a woman who reminds him of his mother. He could be drawn to her, desperate for the kind of stability he lacked when little; perhaps he wants to shower her with kindness to prevent the kind of abuse he got from his mother. He might just begin a cycle of flattering her and giving to her, then pulling back in hurt when it doesn't get him the results he hoped for. As said elsewhere, he's rather liable to end up with a woman as pathologically unpredictable as his mother is or was, this time as an adult man in a relationship that swings between sloppy emotions and flattery, and arguments with silences. Some victims look for someone as unlike their defective caregiver as can possibly be: this too is an escape-strategy that is likely to bring insecurity and instability to the relationship, underlain by a terrible fear of losing that caring other, that antidote to their sickness.

The differences between healthy bonding in a relationship, friendship, even a business venture, have been spelled out. They've been contrasted for you with the powerful addiction-symptoms and feelings of trauma-bonding, and the characteristics of a trauma-bonded relationship. The origins of this trauma have also been explained.

Maybe this leaves you feeling a little ashamed of yourself. Maybe you have some healthier, happier links to some of your family and friends, and these people have been pointing out to you that your relationship is toxic. You are beginning to see how they might be right, and it hurts. Or lastly, you might be that family member, knowing that your loved one is in a toxic relationship and now understanding more of what he she went through in childhood, and why it happened - and you, too, feel ashamed. Why could you not have seen this before? Wasn't there something you could've done?

Remember that we human beings are complicated, and that none of us is perfect. It's quite natural that these reactions happen, irrational as they are, at an age when we just cannot know better. There is no reason to be ashamed: you are not to blame. You will need help, but the help is something you deserve, not something you should be able to do without. You cannot simply sort yourself out. This is not to say that other people can do everything for you: you yourself will have to make some decisions to be equipped to get out of a trauma-bond, either with the other person still in it, if he or she is willing to grow and change, or else away from and free of that person, if not. Those decisions will do you good!

Here is a place to give a word of advice to men. Men are far less likely than women to seek professional help when they are the victims of a trauma-bond or any other stressful situation. We are wired for a certain type of competitiveness and protectiveness. An independent streak abides in most of us, a tendency to hide things; even occasionally to hide the independent streak! A passive, lonely 'Mummy's boy' often seems to have no will to break free of his smothering, overprotective mother - until you know him better. It's there. Maybe it smoulders in the form of an anger turning inwards to depression. That depression might look like total passivity, but it's not. It's hidden anger, and you may just see it flare out occasionally. Men also need help, and they also have no reason to feel ashamed of the scars of their youth. Scarred, poorly-bonded men often father scarred, poorly-bonded children, especially sons! Father doesn't give, because he never got; and he still hasn't learned to bond healthily. All of mankind starts learning how to love very early in life, whether well or badly; but we shall never stop learning. In fact, we don't stop, precisely because loving in all its forms is what life's about!

Chapter 4
Abuse - Ten Questions to Ask Yourself

P reviously, when we looked at what trauma bonds are, and how they can happen to people who have been deprived or mistreated in childhood, the point was made that not all of those people, now in adulthood, are dealing with an abuser deliberately setting out to damage them, or lock them in an emotional jail for that abuser's own good. You might be someone who's ended up with a fellow-patient in life's hospital, or just someone with a partner who has serious attitude problems, or suffers from some psychological weakness.

The unpleasant fact is, though, that many traumatized people, abused or neglected in childhood, do meet abusers and think they've fallen in love with them. We covered the reasons why they might be drawn to abusers, and why the abusers might be drawn to them.

The next two chapters deal specifically with deliberate 'narcissistic' abuse. To achieve the aim of this book it is necessary to explain what it is like and why it happens, and why its victims are affected as they are. If it is bad to be in a trauma bond, to be in a trauma bond with a narcissistic sociopath is worse! If it is confusing to make sense of a muddle of awful feelings, to make sense of a deliberate a mess of awful feelings is harder! This is one of the reasons why there are many questions asked, to help people to see dangers which are not always easy for them to shed light on.

You shudder - "Am I really my partner's prey?" you may be asking. We said we were here to help you. If you are here on behalf of someone else, the same. Without panicking, let us now examine ten questions to ask yourself to find out if you are a victim of abuse by a narcissist.

ONE: Do you make excuses for your partner? This was mentioned before. Do you almost punish yourself because of his or her behavior, saying that you should have known how to handle him or her, should have understood better?

TWO: Do you want to go back to the way the relationship was at the beginning? Was that beginning exciting, lovely-feeling, sexually- and emotionally-intoxicating if it was a romantic relationship, a relief that finally you'd found who you were looking for, maybe? You were being love-bombed, and now it couldn't be more different. Now your partner is critical, difficult, cold, obviously bored with you. Are you thinking that the love-bomber was your real partner; and that this cruel, conflicting one you feel restless in the presence of now, is somehow not the real person you've ended up living with?

THREE: Do you think that if you improved yourself, were more successful, made even more effort to be affectionate, generally just tried harder, that your partner would respond by being faithful, more loving, less critical?

FOUR: Do you keep on because there are a few brief moments of happiness, a few days of good behavior on the part of your spouse or partner? Do you live for them? Do you try to find out what you did to deserve them, so you could have at least a few more 'eyes in your hurricane'?

FIVE: Do you say to yourself that it's too late to change? That you'd love to get out of this, but it's too difficult? That you've put in too much of your time, of yourself, to leave it behind?

SIX: Have you ever found yourself believing that it is actually DANGEROUS to try to leave? That your partner would retaliate by harming you physically? What about fearing that he or she will be so enraged that you won't be able to cope with the strain? Do you fear that he or she will try to blackmail you if you left, tell lies or secrets about you?

SEVEN: Do you feel as if you've lost everything? Can you look back on your life and say, "I used to have more friends; I used to have more fun; I used to feel more confident"? Do you feel that life is much worse now than it was? Is the money running out, so to say, or maybe that's actually true and it feels like it?

EIGHT: Do you think that no-one will want you now, now that you're so depressed, maybe so old, ugly, and carrying a baggage of problems? That you're just not lovable any more?

NINE: Are you still persevering because you believe you'll find a way to make this relationship work? Do you think you'll have a breakthrough that will make your partner a better person; and you, able to manage him or her better?

TEN: Do you hate yourself now? If you always did, do you hate yourself more than you ever did before? Or have you just started liking yourself less and less during the history of this relationship?

Answering in the affirmative to even a few of these questions shows that you are trauma-bonding to that partner... and throwing yourself open to being abused. It is time for us turn these ten questions into some themes seen from an abuser's point of view.

Trauma bonding is like good bonding in that it grows stronger with time. We make this clear: the goal of an abuser is to control the victim, and he or she will aim to increase that control over time. Narcissists play mental games and sow confusion; they take advantage of the natural cycle of conflict and reconciling that occurs in unhealthy relationships, to train their victims to serve them, to use up all their energy in that service. They themselves are, by definition, obsessed with and dedicated to their own desires, utterly unconcerned with the other person's needs.

The narcissistic cycle of abuse involves their infamous 'love-bombing' of the victim, contrasting with mental or physical violence or threats. It's not a stable cycle, but meant to sink down into lower levels when the rewards - the little displays of love, the stopping of hostility - become fewer, and the punishments, greater. The punishments are there to force the victim to do the abuser's will, to be concerned with what that will might be, to exert themselves to please the abuser. The rewards are SOMETIMES given to the victim when he or she carries out the narcissist's wishes.

Sociopathic abuse in a relationship is doubly-damaging because, confused and wrapped-up in the abuser's life, oddly enough wrapped-up again into themselves, victims start to abuse themselves. They question and doubt their goodness or intentions, memorize the often-repeated accusations of their abusers, and their distraction uses up the energy they need to look after themselves. How many things we say or think to ourselves in private - and when a large part of those are negative thoughts about ourselves, how much negativity we will hear!

Throughout the pattern of abuse, you will see a note of criticism, criticism and more criticism. Narcissists start by complaining that their victim makes mistakes, that their work is defective, that their appearance isn't good enough. Nothing is too small to be picked out and judged. Motives are always assumed to be bad, the victim's intelligence rubbished, and his or her achievements belittled. For example, a wife forgets to buy their child a present; the husband explains it by saying that she doesn't care enough about the child. Her knowledge of nature and the environment is called "what she read about in picture-books"; her article published in the local newspaper is printed because "they never have enough real news to fill the paper"!

Abusive treatment and apparent rewards can also be given in public. It has to be acknowledged that narcissists do not manipulate just their victims, and do not just manipulate in private. They are often skilled actors in the presence of other people who could be significant to their victims, a significance of which they are conscious, and which they are afraid of. 'Love-bombing' could take the form of gushing, syrupy thanks given to a partner at a dinner or family gathering; just as likely, the victim could be put down in public: "You'll never guess what my wife believes... she thinks we ought to be eating insects for protein!" Such stratagems could be almost invisibly small: a kiss blown to her boyfriend when they are eating in public at a restaurant where they know the staff, a roll of the eyes when she talks to his father about his difficulties with organizing his time, and she says ironically, "He has been known to be late for work..." All of these actions are designed to build up sympathy for the abuser, and to blacken the character of the victim. A narcissist's public acting serves to distance his or her victim from other people, so that they are less likely to support or defend that victim. It also hides the fact that abuse is taking place. Sadly, such plotting is often successful.

Criticism of the victim in private serves to make that victim feel unlovable, to break the victim down. Doesn't that risk making the victim run away from the relationship? No: if you are unlovable, so the story is told, then nobody else would bear with you the way I have to... Sometimes a narcissist paints a picture of himself or herself as the hero, the suffering one who has to go around picking up all the pieces, even though it is monstrously the other way round! This is another aspect to the devaluing and confusing of the victim: not only is the victim wrong if she complained that her abuser is spending all the money; but the abuser claims to be the frugal one. The victim, she's told, is the one who's wasting money! The next day the abuser comes in sight with vast bags of shopping and quips pleasantly, "Well, we all have to buy our daily bread!" and looks for agreement... from her victim!

Take a moment and match this kind of behavior with that of a loving partner, spouse or friend. If you hit the back of your car on a concrete pole, he or she feels sorry for you, asks if you are unhurt, hopes that it won't be too expensive to fix quickly. If you fail an examination, they feel pain as well, and try to comfort you. If your apples are contaminated with rust mildew, isn't he sorry to hear, and then at once he offers to spray them with fungicide for you?

The abusive partner, spouse, "friend"? calls you a .... idiot when you damage your car. In fact, is more worried about the car than about you; declares that you should have known better what you were letting yourself in for when you decided to study for the exam; and says, "Don't come to me looking for sympathy: every year I hear you complaining about mildew, and every year you don't spray it. What do you think will happen?"

Think of this contrast! Fix yourself on it! Maybe you're the bystander, who's been having the wool pulled over your eyes by a cruel manipulator, abusing someone you know, and sometimes right in front of you! You will have seen the abuser's total lack of real support for his or her victim, even if you have heard the abuser claim to be supporting them. Don't people who love one another help each other? Don't they ignore the usual, agreed pattern of "I cook at weekends" when their loved one is sick, and step in willingly on Tuesday, without having to insist, "That means, of course, I won't be cooking this Saturday. You owe me one."

The criticism of a narcissist is not caused by genuine irritation, or by a moment's tiredness. Mr. Ne'er-Do-Well actually enjoys tearing apart everything his daughter does. He seems quite calm when he tells everyone that she can't even cook water without burning it, that she tried going to a dietitian and never lost weight, that she'll never find a husband. He really isn't spending any sleepless nights wondering if his daughter will ever leave home, because, quite simply, he wants her to stay there. She's serving him better than his late wife ever did! Narcissists will try to find sympathy at every turn. Their overwhelming opinion of themselves makes them feel entitled, jealous, sorry for themselves...

...and that you're undeserving, spoiled, ungrateful, and that YOU shouldn't feel sorry for yourself!!
Are you beginning to see WHY you've been treated badly, HOW it has worked against you, and just how BAD your treatment has been? If this is the case for you, you will see that deep down, you were aware that something like this was happening, though maybe you were ashamed to think so critically of someone else. Ironic, hey?

This monster is the real person you've bonded with in your trauma; the love-bomber is a fictional character! You're not Superman or Wonderwoman, and you cannot fix them. To think they could just be picked up and opened, have a new battery put inside and they'd work properly, is a delusion. Give them the respect due to a human person: they have made choices, and you can't unmake them. Oh, and get yourself to a place where you get some respect... Have you had ANY respect recently?

IMPORTANT: you may feel that you can't leave your relationship because you are in physical danger, that you would be unsafe. Some abusers are purely threateners, but sometimes you know there is a real possibility that your safety would be at risk. It is true, one has to admit, that an abuser can become unpredictable when his or her plans to enslave you threaten to come to an end, because you have left. Please, plan and think of a way to find a safe place, if that is the case. You will need help!

Chapter 5
You're in Love with the Trauma Bond, not the Narcissist!

Y es, this is what people trapped emotionally in an abusive relationship with a narcissistic sociopath have to realize: they're in love with the trauma bondage, and not the person they think they love!

It sounds crazy, but it isn't. In this chapter it will be explained to sufferers what has happened, so that they can see and understand themselves better, from yet another angle. For those who are seeking to inform themselves so as to help a loved one or acquaintance, this concept is introduced as being news they need to break gently but firmly to the one they are trying to help.

You're not really, genuinely in love. You might believe you are, passionately - and let us just be reminded that the word 'passion' means 'suffering', in any case - but love is a cake made of several ingredients. To keep with this example: if there is no flour, then you could put all the other ingredients (baking powder, water, sugar, butter, vanilla essence...) into the mix, but it wouldn't be bakeable into a cake! If, in your relationship, you are treated as an inferior... if respect is totally lacking... If the butter's left out, what does the cooked lump come out as? If no water were used, wouldn't you get some kind of rock...?! Do you see what this means? (By the way, one can be sure a narcissist will never forget the vanilla essence, even if she "forgot" the sugar!)

Love simply implies accepting, respecting, dealing honestly. What doesn't have these things, isn't love. Yes, it is true that we use the word 'love' to describe all sorts of powerful feelings (positive and negative) that can be experienced in relationships. Truly, 'love' is an over-used word. To think of it! We say, almost glibly, "I love my Mom; I love my Dad"; and then, "I love fried chicken"!!

Declaring your feelings to someone, saying that you're in love with them, certainly re-enforces those feelings. It is a fact that what you confess by speaking about it, is strengthened inside you. That is normally a good thing; but as with any good thing, it can go off-course. Strengthening those intense feelings doesn't make them become real love.

In the heart of real love is trust. When you love someone, not only do you love them because you trust them, you love them because they trust you. It must be mutual. If you really found love with a narcissistic personality, that individual would trust you and by implication, open up to you. You have to allow people to love you. Remember the aspect of shared vulnerability, mentioned earlier in the chapter on human bonding? Hold on - a narcissist is not willing to be vulnerable! To him or to her, that is weakness. And power, not weakness, is the object of a narcissist's entering into any kind of relationship. Even a magazine subscription! How much more, a supposedly intimate link between two people.

If you are a victim of an abuser, you are being controlled by that abuser. In an intimate relationship with, probably, a sexual side to it, the abuser will try to tell you that you are in love with him or her - that you are weak (at the knees) for him or her - for no other reason than to get power over you. That power will be wielded by means of a little bit of pleasure - and a lot of pain.

Your first technicolor feelings for your narcissist, if you are a victim, were of an attraction to the mysterious, the unknown. Certainly, you cannot have known that person, because you cannot have foreseen how horrible and painful your relationship was going to become. Not so? Have you ever caught yourself saying, "If only I'd known what I was letting myself in for! If only I could have seen ahead to the pain and loss I feel now! I'd never have done it..." You were on your best behavior, anxious to please, and so was the narcissist. You were open to new experiences, and so was he or she; but a little while later, invisibly, the abuser shut himself or herself in emotionally, and began to take advantage of you. You were still open emotionally, and so it became like taking candy from a baby, so to say.

Maybe the first shock was brief, but sudden. For example, the widow who marries a monster will come to him one day, a month or two later, to ask for money for her children's clothing. Something she's done before, and had a generous response to... He suddenly snaps at her: "They're not my children. Why do you think I'm going to pay for them?" He might be loving again later that very day, but soon another attack or denial is going to follow. The cycle of abuse has started, and before long, his insults, criticism and infidelity will outweigh all of his apparent generosity or friendliness.

Such a person will know that his first affection is being missed. He will use that memory again and again to make you come running after him. You may not even suffer a sudden, first shock such as the one just pictured: instead, he might just seem to become gradually less enthusiastic, colder, more withdrawn. You are being accustomed to going without 'love' for periods of time, because in his entitlement-obsessed, selfish, greedy inner person, you have to merit his little gifts. You have to balance the ball on your nose, longer and longer, before he will throw you a tiny sardine!

You are being trauma-bonded, slowly but surely. Meanwhile, the drugs you've been fed - personal attention, sex, space to think of your ideal future, sharing your daydreams (and, once you go without them: gut-wrenching pain, anxiety, restlessness, depression and all) - are a cocktail more addictive than cocaine! Your BODY is hooked as much as is your mind. Why did we just use the words, 'gut-wrenching'? We could have added, 'heart-ache', 'stomach-churning', 'head-spinning', being 'stabbed in the back', for that's how it feels. Your body is as controlled, your hormones affected as much as is your reason. Your drug-pusher has you trapped, so that you have to buy his or her drug!

It's drugs, not proper hugs... Herein lies the reason that victims of abuse feel so much pain. They will have to understand and come out of their deception, to see that they are not in love. That realization must happen before they can begin to heal themselves and be healed with the help of others. Inside, every victim has to go back to something that was almost always heard deep within at the beginning of their first negative experiences of a sociopath, possibly even before: a sense or intuition of some of that person's words and actions not being right, of facts being changed, flashes of less pleasant emotions, remarks revealing unexpected malice, perhaps ill-will to someone or something else. The victim decided to switch it off, to ignore it. Now he or she must return there mentally, and needs to feel that uncertainty and lack of peace again. It was a warning, and not nearly as painful as the result of not heeding it. So go ahead, don't be frightened to feel it!

The truth may hurt, but it always heals. These words will be heard again and again when you have to deal with inner pain. It is also true that the truth hurts narcissists, but the difference is that they don't let it heal them. Narcissists avoid real confrontation with the truth, because they are cowards. The best example is this: unfaithful spouses often hide their affairs with apparent total calm. How unlike them to open up and confess to you if they can keep on getting away with it! They are liars, consummate, brilliant liars, because they lie with such calm. The truth is so unimportant to them, and yet so awkward, that they stay away from it. They are used to the world of lies, and lying doesn't cause the tension in them that it would in you, or any other flawed-but-normal individual. That is the tragic reason why you and so many other people believe their lies, for a time at least. If anyone manages to expose their crimes, they may find themselves in a frantic argument or side-issue, because the narcissist is trying to get away from the subject, away from the thing he or she hates: the truth.

Having an affair, for a narcissist who is filled with bad pride and a sense of entitlement, is something he or she deserves. It's probably good for their health, they would say! For a victim, it is very different. A common situation that causes trauma bonding is when a victim (one of them...) is enticed to have a love-affair with a married or otherwise committed - bonded - abuser. How many people in the whole world have heard that the abusive partner was GOING to leave the existing spouse, the 'old' lover, and the abuser never did! Once more, lies are told: lies, lies, lies. The warning in this case is clear, but so often a traumatized person isn't strong enough to hold back, chooses to take the risk and ignore it, only to suffer later. Once the affair has started, the trauma bond and its extreme pain make the thought of putting right what is wrong become almost unbearable.

This is not a condemnation. Something wrong has been done, but that can't be changed by pointing fingers. To be healed, however, is to go back mentally to the intuition of danger, or the visible, logical, calm reasons why the affair was a breaking of someone else's promises. If the abuser really loved the new person with whom he or she started to have an affair, then why had he or she not already left the previous spouse or lover? Doesn't it take time to let go of someone emotionally? (As you are learning how to do!!!) Can you have peace in that situation? No. A narcissist doesn't care about peace as much as about power and pleasure. The truth may hurt, but it heals. Sometimes circumstances do just that: when the victim, also cheating as we just saw, yet still hoping for the whole and complete commitment he or she has been promised umpteen times, that victim who really wants to put it right, finds out that the abuser has actually been carrying on not only with him or her, but with someone else as well! Maybe even more people! That shock of awakening could actually be more healing than it will feel at first. However, the victim has to decide to want to be awakened. Victims can't hope that someone or some situation like this will do it for them.

Narcissists leave not just a victim, but many. In that example of affairs and adulteries, there are always at least two victims. How late it is in this book not to have to mentioned children! Children in a relationship which is a trauma bond, whether the children of one partner from a previous relationship, or children born to the abuser and victim, are civilian casualties in the midst of a furious war. They will be victims too, whether abused with cruelty, ignored, or used as tools to curry favor and love. One of the greatest causes of trauma in childhood is growing up in a home with a narcissist parent or step-parent. Just as children grow up and have their own children, abusers and victims risk bringing up the next generation of abusers and victims; taught by poor wretched victims how to be poor wretched victims, or egged on to do anything not to be (maybe to become abusers instead?). Or taught by cruel, heartless villains how to be cruel heartless villains, otherwise egged on to any length not to be, including allowing themselves to become victims instead? What do you think?

With regard to children in a relationship: their safety is important, but for all the same reasons yours is, plus their vulnerability. They are not a reason to sacrifice your happiness in a case of trauma bonding, for their own happiness and well-being is also in danger. Isn't a home supposed to be a place of safety for a child? So, even if you have children, the process of breaking the trauma bonds that hold you prisoner is not different, though they may make it sometimes harder, sometimes easier for you, a parent, to let go of an abuser.

Using children as tools can go to the extremes of a narcissist abusing them sexually or torturing them mentally. You, an adult, are sensitive. How sensitive do you think small children are? This ill-treatment born out of total hard-heartedness or bitter jealousy involving little ones, is one of the greatest of all evils. Picture the jealous mother who pushes her child to sit down in front of the fireplace, and in that fireplace burns up the presents the child's father has just given for his birthday, hissing, "He doesn't love you, he doesn't love you! He's just a liar!" Narcissist sociopaths are evil. So how, how can you fall in love with someone who is evil?

Chapter 6
Trauma and Your Body

T he way trauma affects the human body almost like a drug, a drug with terrible withdrawal-symptoms, has already been presented to the reader of this book. The healing process from a trauma-bonded relationship will get a lot of help when you learn to become aware of your body, and to take part in physical or mental activities that overcome the stress you suffer. The advice here is not, obviously, professional medical advice, but is given to encourage you to take part in some healthy activities.

We carry trauma around with us when we suffer it, in its bodily effects. It makes us sigh, gives us headaches, makes our hearts beat faster. We know that.

Headaches are triggered when we are tense. Sometimes our jaw is clenched tight, or our head held in such a way that it affects the circulation, and that can set off a headache. If the heart is beating faster because we're stressed, the blood vessels in our heads pound and we feel it as throbbing pain.

The heart beats faster when we strain physically and exert our bodies more, but also even when we don't do any hard physical exercise, but suffer from stress. Exercising to make the heart work faster is usually good for a normal healthy person, but stressing and getting the heart all worked up while we just sit or stand is not good for us. It makes blood pressure go up, but for nothing.

Some people sweat copiously when anxious: their foreheads run, palms sweat, and most of their skin puts out more moisture. We vary. How many of us, though, remember rushing with a rucksack or backpack in an airport to get to a 'plane, and once seated inside, realized that we were soaked? Sweating with exercise is usually healthy; sweating with stress is not the same, as well as being unpleasant.

Our muscles tighten when we are suffering stress. People in a state of trauma suffer all of these physical effects so often over time that their bodies almost mold themselves into bent, tightened positions. Shoulders and neck bend over, hands clench, muscles around our lungs pull tight; even our swallowing can become difficult.

Swallowing reminds us of the stomach. The first thing stress and tension do to the stomach is to make us eat too fast, in some cases. Or people may just lose their appetite; others eat to try to make themselves feel better. Another effect is that when we experience tension, it also causes our stomachs to produce more acid; and combined with not eating enough, or eating too fast, or too much (paradoxically) we start suffering from indigestion. Problems such as stomach ulcers, IBS, vomiting, constipation, diarrhea and the like are not caused just by stress. However, it certainly can make them worse!

The way to heal yourself from these and other physical side-effects of trauma is not just to exercise, or to concentrate and relax - of course, these are good and shall be dealt with soon - but consists in re-connecting your body with your mind. Growing up in a dysfunctional environment and suffering trauma can make a child separate his or her thoughts and feelings from the world, including, very importantly, the body. Why? It's an attempt to protect ourselves. Thoughts and sensations may be far from totally obedient to the will, but the physical world is much less controllable to someone who is young. They might try to flee from it, into an imaginary world. At the same time, thoughts of pain and confusion actually distract them from their bodies, and the physical symptoms of their stress are just allowed to happen. Physical symptoms can seem unpredictable, so a child doesn't try to understand them so as to alleviate them; or they can seem inevitable, uncontrollable, and thus not worth tackling.

So whatever we can do in our bodies to relieve ourselves from trauma will involve feeling their sensations and learning how to be aware of them again, re-connecting them to our thoughts. Exercises that stretch and relax the parts of the body mentioned as being vulnerable to tension, will help. A session in the gym can help one to stop worrying and concentrate instead on one's body, thus relaxing the mind. Yoga and other practices of calm can help us to focus. Breathing techniques, practised not just in yoga but in other methods, are a way for us to be aware of our need for fresh air, and to breathe it in the best way.

Healthy eating and good exercise will make our bodies feel better, and thus help a victim of a traumatic relationship to feel less depressed. Foods we actually crave when depressed can even be the type of food to avoid if we want to get better. Craving the 'rush' of lots of sugar has an effect similar to a drug for some: they feel pleasure, but afterwards, once blood-sugar falls again, there is an unpleasant sensation. It's also a cycle, and can also be addictive! Like breaking the trauma bond itself, it takes time to re-learn how to look after your body, but as you begin to do so, your mood will improve!

Being under stress for a long time makes our bodies' hormones overwork. We feel as if we are going to be in a fight (and in a trauma bond, you probably were...) which increases certain hormones, or else, being beaten into mental submission, we try to avoid abuse, setting off all the 'flight' sensations of wanting to run away (sometimes doing just that) and stimulating the production of those hormones instead. Such hormones are produced rapidly in nature to help us in short, dangerous situations. Instead, abuse-victims produce them over long periods. Relaxation and healthy living can adjust our hormones to a good balance and healthier levels.

Chapter 7
More Signs and Characteristics of Trauma Bonding

W hen you read the title of this chapter, you may have wondered why it would be necessary, seeing that we've already dealt with some ways to know if your relationship, or that of someone you know, is a trauma bond. Haven't we finished with this?

Perhaps you have indeed decided that you are in a trauma bond, or that you are definitely not. Yet we have to re-iterate that for many people, this overwhelming and painful experience, coupled with the deliberate confusion of an abuser, is very hard to see and understand. It makes victims question their judgment endlessly, or avoid making judgments out of fear of being wrong! We are here to help, and so provide some more detailed descriptions to assist you to see where you stand. Throughout the book you will read or hear many examples and descriptions, some of which may help you a lot more than others. We are all slightly different, all individuals. Yet the stories of other sufferers' lives, their testimonies, show that we are dealing with a problem that is found all over the world, and was known through history. To hear these stories and understand them is liberating. Age-old wisdom combined with modern insights can shed light on your solutions.

Two words used in the description of abusive manipulation need to be explained for those who don't know them: STONEWALLING and GAS-LIGHTING.

'Stonewalling' is the attitude, almost like a process, that begins after the apparently loving and affectionate first stage of a narcissistic relation-ship. The sudden or gradual withdrawing of attention, the closing-off of that person's inner thoughts and feelings. Conversation about this change is refused; apparent problems are just avoided. The abuser will no longer communicate as an equal, so the victim will feel that there's a change in authority, though not know why. Literally, it's as if he or she discovers a stone wall between much of the abuser's life and their own.

'Gaslighting' is when an abuser makes a victim start self-questioning and doubting their own knowledge or judgment. Secretly, victims are being confused, their version of events denied, their memory questioned. This includes even the fact of their being attacked verbally or physically! Victims end up in a state of constant anxiety, debating to themselves if things actually happened as they did. Perhaps they try to decide if they are being abused, or not! This helps a lot to explain why they are aware that they have problems in their relationships, yet they cannot see what is happening to them. They are left in a state of not being able to make assertive, positive decisions, staying on and on when they should be getting out. If that is you: again, don't beat yourself down because it happened to you, and don't hate yourself. What you should see is that it's deliberate. Your abuser WANTS you to think his or her mistreatment is "all in your head"... You have the verbal picture from the words 'gas' and 'light' of an old-fashioned gas-powered lamp. It gives off a weak and odd-colored light, unlike daylight, and makes distances and objects hard to judge accurately. That is the symbolism of the expression.

Backing up an abuser's strategy of confusing his or her victim, is an effort to isolate the victim from other relationships. Limiting contact with friends or family is a way to remove not only sympathy for the victim, not only moral support, not only a way to hide the abuser's bad treatment, but it is a way to keep him or her confused. One of the remedies of being gaslighted is to speak to other people, to get their opinions and see their viewpoints. That is the way we form, change and keep our beliefs and opinions. We share them. We agree with people. Or we agree to disagree. Narcissists know this and fear it; they strive to keep their victims on their own, living "inside their own heads".

Narcissistic abuse is serious. It's far more than just emotional unpleasantness. Punching, tormenting with sharp objects, being threatened with knives or guns, forced sex, being imprisoned physically in a house or room, have all happened to people, nearly all women. Yes, men have been threatened with violence or suffered it, at the hands of paid thugs or angry family-members; or poisoned, blackmailed, or forced to the courts of law again and again. And still some of these victims are saying, "But I still love him/her"!! Some of them actually return, of their free will, to such situations!

Nothing in these descriptions of an abuser suggests that, clever though he or she might be, an abuser is all-knowing or all-powerful. Being totally self-obsessed and always sorry for oneself, being selfish and jealous, is not good for them, just as they aren't good for anyone. The lives and characters of all abusers will start going into a downward spiral. A number of sociopathic personalities are alcoholics or drug addicts. Alcohol doesn't just make them violent, or make them lose self-control in speech or words: used to excess, it damages their brains permanently and twists their thoughts and judgments. Abusers can, therefore, be deeply trapped in delusions. A man may accuse his wife of having many affairs - when in reality he's held her prisoner in their house, and accompanied her on every shopping-trip, for months! Of course, many abusers do know the truth of what they falsely accuse their victims of. On this account they are liars. However, lies and alcohol combined, being what they are, have made some abusers completely delusional.

This is not a reason to feel sorry for them, in the way used so glibly to mean, 'excuse'. If they are narcissists, they got into their ugly state out of their own fault. And it does not change the fact that they cause harm, that in fact they are some of the more dangerous and unpredictable of abusers. You have to protect yourself. You need to live in a safe place. Then, you also need to break the invisible chains inside you - the trauma bonds. That may take longer.

What follows is meant especially for people who are no longer living with an abusive partner. It doesn't matter whether it was because they've been 'dumped' and he or she left; or because, for example, a wife has had to flee from the relationship because she was being attacked and beaten physically, and now lives away. If there was a trauma bond with that person, then it is probably still there. Time does heal, but without help and understanding, it can be very slow. It's really tragic to think of the widow whose husband abused her, still saying, "I'll always love him," years after he's dead, and still not getting on with her life.

So: are any of the following true for you...?

Firstly: do you wish your partner would come back, traumatic though it almost always was to live with that person? Do you think you might have made a mistake to leave? You put off making changes because you know he or she might not approve... For example, a woman thinks of sending her child away to a boarding school. He'll be safer from the abusive father there, and the standard of education will be better. Yet she procrastinates, puts off changing his school, because she knows that his father wouldn't agree, would fly into a rage if she sent their boy away. Even though she's left the boy's father. Her life still continues as if he's renting a part of it!

Secondly: you are an abused partner whose 'ex' is trying to invite you back. You are being love-bombed, and told how very sorry he or she is about the past bad treatment. Promises are being made, kind words said. You were abused, truly mistreated - but you find there are times when you want to believe what you are hearing. Maybe not all the time, but sometimes you feel a pull to go back and try again. You start wondering if this "new leaf" your 'ex' has turned might not be genuine, and thinking about the terms under which you'd go back to him or to her. Is that you?

Thirdly: do still catch yourself making excuses for your partner's behavior in what is now the past? Do you say to yourself that you must be at least partly to blame for the insults, criticisms, infidelities and attempts to 'gaslight' you, that you endured? It's true, no-one's perfect; but if you hardly ever returned his insults, didn't dare to criticize him for things in his own life, were never unfaithful, and never tried to confuse him... how is it that you're trying to share the blame for his doing that to you?

Fourthly: there is still a kind of emotional "connection" between you. If you hear news of your former partner, for example when his shop in town puts on a promotion and people are talking about it, does it really stir your emotions? As it would obviously do if you were still living with him? Do you find that, uncannily, you are reminded of him so strongly, for example, when you hear an expression he used to use... and then within an hour he's sent you an SMS text message? So that it seems there's a connection still there, that's as if it MUST be, even though part of you knows that you need to break it off? You'll need to make a conscious decision to break free...

Fifthly: you keep on thinking the way your narcissist wanted you to. Ideas and assertions that person made still seem to sway you at times. For example, her strong views that street-market vendors are all crooks and confidence-tricksters still keep repeating themselves noisily in your head every time you go to look at a street-market, and you find yourself looking suspiciously at all their goods. You might fight against it, but you can't stop feeling it is so, even though your reason tells you it's unfair and generalizing.

Sixthly: you think a lot about your ex-partner. Everything reminds you of that person. You remember so much of his or her past injustices that it's like feeling it all over again. You wish you could have avoided what happened, re-plan it, imagine what you should have done... To remember is, of course, part of understanding, and so to be healed, some analysis is called for; but this kind of memory is passive, and it is making you feel helpless and bitter about the past.

If these things were once true and are no longer, then you are healed. If they are the case in your life, then it is most likely that you are stuck in a trauma bond. However, again we repeat: it was a natural process that happened to get you into this mess. There is a natural process of healing, and healing is truly possible. Just make sure that you get help; with guidance it will be much easier. And do not try to punish yourself because of what's happened!

The help you will need to break out of your inner prison can be found in different ways. If you have family and friends who are at least sympathetic, that is a start; though many victims have been distanced from family and friends, perhaps deliberately and successfully by their abusers, or have drifted apart from them beforehand, so they were vulnerable prey to an abuser at the beginning.

Professional counselors and psychologists who specialize in healing from abusive relationships can deal with you in compassion, and using their knowledge. They've made it their work to help people in your situation.

Support-groups are another way to meet people and get help. Unlike your family, they've been through exactly what you did. If you are a family-member of an abused person, they would be able to explain to you what has been happening to him or her. Such groups advertise themselves and hold meetings. Nowadays they can be joined by means of the internet and social media, so that you don't have to worry if there is no such group near you! You are NOT alone.

Chapter 8
The Emotional Dynamics of Trauma-Bonding

T here are different understandings and schools of thought concerning the way that trauma bonds affect our interaction with other people, and explanations as to why traumatized people tend to attract abusive personalities to themselves. In this chapter we will touch on some observations. Some of these theories of why people behave in relationships in the way they do are quite speculative, and concern themselves with the spiritual aspect of a human person. In this book we will not go into this in detail, keeping more to a psychological point of view; but it is so important to realize the essential agreement that all these beliefs have in common - that you need to break free; that you have been mistreated; that you will be healed by being healed from within yourself; and that healing is possible.

Some psychologists point to the need for people in abusive relationships to release themselves from emotional and 'energy' connections which are diseased. The theory goes like this: every person has an energy-field around him or her, a bubble of activity and life coming from within, from the human soul. Our emotional woundedness is like having holes or weak points in it. Those who follow psychologists such as C.J.Jung see two types of energy within our souls: male and female. Female energy attracts the energy of other people to itself; male energy seeks to find the energy of others and give to it. They are opposites and yet similar. Both types of this energy are found in both sexes, not being restricted to one, though there seems to be a balance in favor of male energy in most men, and female in most women.

If someone's emotional wounds, let us say of childhood, are the same kind as those of another, then the male energy will 'fit' into the wound of the female energy's sphere of operation. When she is with him, for example, a woman will feel as if she's being healed and balanced. However, when he goes away or there is some kind of conflict between them, or if he draws back (whether deliberately or not), her energy will move to her masculine, and she will start to 'chase' him and seek him. This is the analogy.

The more similar are the wounds of the couple, the more intense this feeling and effect will be. If it is only with regard to some particular experience of life and not a great number of traumas, then the feeling will be lesser.

What happens? When people feel this sense of loss because there is serious conflict in their relationship, or their partner has left, they want that other person intensely. It is a tragedy that many counselors and psychologists are trying to help these victims to be re-united with their partners, even though, in their woundedness, that is the last thing they need!

You will need to heal your wounds for yourself. This is in agreement with all that was said prior to this chapter. One of the main sources of our conflicts is found in our suffering in childhood. Yet, if you reconcile yourself with what happened, understand and come to terms with it, you will come to the point where your family, living or dead, will not upset you any more. You will no longer allow them to anger you with your memories of their actions in the past, or allow them to carry on devaluing you. When that emotional balance happens, you will have been released from emotional bondage to them. You will need to remember what happened, and picture yourself, now adult, explaining and loving yourself in that situation. You need to make yourself feel loved in that time when you weren't.

A striking observation made by people who follow the school of energy-dynamics is this: if you can be healed and set free from the wounds of your life - whatever caused them, and there are some more challenging theories - then you will see a partner you have trauma-bonded with, for who that person really is. Not who you believe they are, or would like them to be... Frankly, most people, they say, fall in love with the PO-TENTIAL of another - not how they actually are!!

For someone trying to help another person to break a trauma bond, a few ideas here may also seem a little difficult to accept. However, you should be able to see the truth of the practical observations made. You can probably see the similarities and differences in the personality of your loved one and the abusive or conflicting partner he or she had. You can encourage them and point out some uncomfortable truths - and some hope-inspiring guidelines, but you cannot force anyone else to be healed and to change. You must insist gently, but firmly, that change will come when they make an inner decision to seek it.

More intuitive theories of interpersonal energy dynamics can invoke the idea of your having influence from having lived other, past lives; and karma, the idea that you have to come to terms with and accept suffering on account of the wrongs committed in those previous lives. Or that tribes, ancestors and nations in your past have had their influence on you. We cannot try to prove these here, but return to the basic agreement of therapists: you need to be healed from within, to be able to resist the influences of people who may seem powerfully attractive, but are NOT right for you. When you can do that, people who are good for you will come to you in their, and your, own time.

RECOVERY SEEN FROM THIS DYNAMIC

Some people use the expression, "your twin-flame" to describe someone who suffers from what you suffer, or to put it more or less as we did at the beginning of this book, a fellow-victim who's fallen into the same swamp as you have. So this is not necessarily a narcissist. Sometimes this is presented as being an ideal person to be with; but whatever words are used, the dynamic of energy in personal relationships shows that he or she is NOT ideal, not good at all. Other people will hear the words, 'your divine soul-connection' and think a fellow-victim is that person. No, counselors should not use those two expressions for this situation. The victim needs help first.

Yes, a victim can find his or her soul-mate, but only once he or she is healed! This is what the dynamics of emotional energy suggest - when

49

you no longer suffer from deep unmet needs and trauma, you will attract the truly compatible type of person to your life, the one whose male or female energy is matched to yours by being opposite. When you do, what heals in your life will heal them. No-one is perfect, but your soul-mate will be someone who wants to grow WITH you. Not FROM you...

When you have become enough for yourself, another suitable person will "mirror" your inner personality, and there will be a sense of peace. You won't need to fight to win them, have to ask them to come into your life with pleading. They will just come near you calmly and your bond will grow, as said before, steadily and slowly.

It's not a 'divine soul-connection' when you cannot stop thinking about someone, when you feel a desperate need to be with them, otherwise you will never have enough. That's not divine: it's a wound!!

Wounded connections start with high energy, and develop quickly - it's been written in this book already - but start to pull apart also very quickly. This tension is excruciating, we've said. Yet when in contrast you are CONTENT, when you feel OK on your own, strangely, you'll draw someone similar but compatible to your inner self, towards you. In peace. You'll be able to have fun together!

You will need to forgive your abuser and perhaps family and friends who didn't understand you. You must forgive - in the sense of letting go of - your abuser. Yet if you have made that decision, but can't stop feeling anger and bitterness, then it shows that you need to continue the process inside. YOU NEED TO FORGIVE YOURSELF AS WELL.

Your instincts, and often the deliberate actions of your abuser, made you hate yourself. That isn't humility. Humility is to accept, and part of that here is to forgive yourself for the crazy things you did. Such as: letting yourself be treated the way you were; not listening to your inner voice telling you that you were in trouble; not listening to warnings from other people; maybe for having had children with your abuser; for not wanting to see that he or she is a narcissist. Be good to yourself and, admitting that you've made mistakes, then let the past go! When you start to heal, you will be able to do this.

You can have a good attitude to your abuser naturally when you have a good attitude to yourself. A good attitude to the abuser here would be to be calm and firm, not feeling a need to punish, or retaliate for the wrong you suffered. It's not any kind of approval of what they did. If you became masochistic, in other words you felt you deserved to be punished by your abuser, and felt a sort of empty pleasure when he or she caused you pain, you must forgive yourself. This attitude is destructive. Remember that the command is: "Love Thy Neighbor as Thyself". That's not the same as, "Love Your Neighbor and Hate Yourself", is it?

We all want to be loved. Women know this very deeply, and so often search frantically for love. But they will find love within themselves, otherwise they will be driven to chase for the potential of someone else, denying their feminine energy, as we have seen.

Actually, say the practitioners who teach the balancing of emotional energy, you set yourself up to be treated badly when you chase after healing from another person. It's uncanny, but the universe seems to provide abusers for victims. "Why?" we might want to protest.

We are all made of light, one could say. It seems that you cannot see yourself as light, however, unless you are in the dark! If you seek something, you will have to go through the opposite of it, so that you can be given the choice to step into what you've been asking for. Your healing journey, even though it didn't seem to be a healing journey when you wanted to chase your answer to prayer, will eventually take you to the place where you can choose and be at peace with what you really need, and whom.

Women who start going out on dates after a traumatic relationship often have the wrong view of their needs. So, ladies, did you worry about your appearance? Did you wonder if he liked your style of conversation? Do you wonder if he will call you or send you a text-message the next day? Your focus is all on HIM. This can warp your judgment. Do you ask for your own sake: "Is he going to value me? Will he respect me? Did he actually notice me?"

You see, if he didn't see you as you are, notice who and what you are, then he can't be right for you. It isn't your job to make other people understand you, pay attention to you, or accept you. YOU need to keep on seeing yourself, seeing the goodness and the value in who you are and what talents you've been given. You're worth it! they say. Then you'll meet someone who sees you. Be honest with yourself: do you enjoy being 'chased' by a former partner? Don't - it's just a waste. But admit to yourself that it tempts you, and that it's crazy - but forgive yourself for thinking crazily, as you start to see how false it is. You are sacred: don't treat yourself as something cheap; don't throw yourself at anyone.

'Chasing' someone or an external solution to your pain is tragic. People can waste years of their lives doing it. Being 'chased' or 'love-bombed' by an abuser also wastes your time. Don't react to it. You live only once, and you can't get years back again... Yet in the presence of someone loving, you can make time seem to slow down as you savor every moment with them. You yourself will have become loving and peaceful beforehand, as you were meant to be, by accepting not your trauma and the ghost it made you love, but yourself accepted and loved, and someone else as he or she really is.

Chapter 9
Trauma Bonds, Stockholm Syndrome and Narcissistic Abuse

S o much of the power that a trauma bond has to confuse its victim lies in the way it re-enforces itself both positively and negatively. The behavior of an abuser is not all bad - the 'Smooth Operator' rewards and praises his victim for a while, sometimes putting quite a lot of effort into his performance, especially at the beginning. We are used to getting rewards from people and from life that are based on what we've done. Then Mr. Smooth Operator turns nasty at other times, maybe violently so. Since childhood, we are also used to getting punishments for our actions or omissions. So a victim will think that it must be possible to control his or her environment with the abuser. After all, abusers often say that they're doing what they do as a reward or as a punishment, even if they are horribly inconsistent.

The victim gets these double reinforcements, and starts trying to please the narcissist. From not going out of their home, to wearing smarter clothes, to waiting before she answers him back... she treads on thin ice, so as not to fall in. This, she hopes, will stop him from coming back home drunk, from hitting her.

The two opposing forces cause the relationship to wobble, you could say, between two violent extremes. Traumatic-bonded couples have a truly "roller-coaster ride" which other people should be able to see. Though the times when the abusive partner is charming may decrease as the relationship is poisoned, and his or her control of the victim increases, this not to deny that some abusers make a lot of effort, as just said. Some of them have been known to give expensive gifts and take their victims on expensive holidays. Some can keep up the effort for quite some time, perhaps during a period of engagement to be married. All of that will not nullify that their abuse and mistreatment can be equally severe!

Normal, healthy relationships just aren't like this. They can seem... boring in comparison. Does this not help to explain why victims can become confused, and stay in unstable relationships too long? Or why a victim who is seduced by a narcissist might find it dull and difficult to remain faithful to their spouse? The good times can, especially at first, be intense.

It makes victims confuse love, truthfulness and honesty with beautiful emotional firework-displays. It can also confuse other people around them as well, since many narcissists like making these displays of affection in public.

This extends not just to rewarding, affectionate behavior, but to acts and displays of sorrow, or gestures such as agreeing to go to marriage-guidance counseling. Floods of tears after an affair must mean genuine regret... not so? So many victims, and so many of their nearest bystanders, even figures of authority, are taken in. Narcissists have a skill in identifying figures of authority to validate what they do in public, and maybe get subtle criticism of their victims heard at a higher level. Yet think! The only sincere apology is a change in someone's behavior...

Victims can get pressure put on them from all sides when an abuser weaves a web around their situation, when other people, even therapists, even friends, have been duped. Once they've been in a cycle of intense trauma-bonding for a long time, they can be completely blind to the difference between feelings and genuine love, and when starved of excitement, they cannot believe that love would feel anything other than what they feel in the apparently good times. People who have understood the way they were blinded to the fact of being abused, and are starting to heal themselves, can sometimes panic and ask themselves why they are attracted to Mr. Smooth Operator types, and not to Mr. Average types. It's because they've been addicted from dose after dose, and withdrawal symptoms after withdrawal symptoms, to feel like this. It will decrease, but will take time. It's not their fault.

Controlling a victim can be presented as caring concern, a desire to 'protect'. In family abuse, this is particularly relevant to abuse of children by a parent or parents. Little Milly may be kept at home almost all the time she is not at school; even there at school, she might have to send text messages to her mother at every break. Her teacher (if she ever gets to see the mother) asks why this constant demand for Milly to use her phone is necessary; maybe also why the mother won't let her daughter play any sports, or take part in any non-academic activities at all. "Ah," says Milly's mother, "but children face so many dangers these days. I do everything I can to make sure she stays safe." Milly is actually an unhappy prisoner in her own home!

STOCKHOLM SYNDROME is a related phenomenon which was named after the incident in Sweden in 1973, when a kidnapper took four people hostage after a failed bank robbery, and with his threats, managed to get an accomplice allowed in to help him. They all spent six days in a bank vault. After their release, the four victims refused to testify in court against their kidnappers, and then started to raise money for their defense. People suspected some sort of brainwashing, but the ringleader denied having any such power or intention, nor is there evidence of it. What happened?

In such a situation, the prisoners were totally dependent on their captors to stay alive, since the men were armed; if they had permission to drink or eat, it was given by their captors. This resembles the pattern of reward and punishment seen in abusive romantic relationships, though in this case it happened very quickly, surprisingly so. Other kidnapping victims have disagreed with this explanation, calling it a logical reaction instead. If you are in danger of death or mutilation and have little ability to protect yourself, and cannot escape, so it goes, it is simply logical to adapt to and be co-operative with your kidnapper. All of that isn't really a disagreement, it must be said. It's still a survival strategy. Such strategies can help us; but if they involve deep and powerful feelings, there is a danger of their becoming irrational and harming rather than protecting their victims.

What does an abusive villain look like? The word 'villain' was used deliberately! One of the dangers of abusive relationships is that societies in general have a false, dramatic picture of what a narcissist looks like. Are they all silent, moody, anti-social, ugly-looking or visibly diseased? Has every one of them been mistreated so badly as a child? The fact is that they can be of many, many different appearances and origins. Often they have strong and individual personalities and can be of handsome or beautiful looks. Their abilities can be totally genuine - Lady Lovincurtains could be genuinely artistic and be able to hold a brilliant conversation at a party. She may give to charity not only in money but of her time. But: she has humiliated and insulted her stuttering husband for twenty years, and has blackmailed him into silence regarding the fact that she hits their daughter with a horsewhip almost every day! It is quite possible that there is, in the case of some abusers, some good will and some better parts to their personalities, that their narcissism is not total. Nor do they abuse all the time.

Not only do we tend to think that abusers must look ugly, we tend to think that there must be places or situations where you'd never find a narcissist. "He's an elder of his church," people say, "respected there for years. How could he do that to little children?" Others are in politics as spokespeople for the rights of others, or as mentioned, belong to charities which raise large amounts of money for the needy. We don't see it. No criticism of these societies or organizations is intended when one might say this, but the unfortunate fact is: that no matter what color your holy cows are, if you have an abuser in your midst, his holy cows always happen to be the same color as yours! There is no social group too holy, too good, or too difficult to infiltrate. This a fact of life; obviously people have to put measures in place to protect others in social groups, but part of that protection is in realizing this fact. Too much abuse has taken place because abusers found a good place to validate themselves by taking advantage of other people or places with a good name.

Keep it simple! The truth of abuse is just that, however complicated the things that hide it. Have you had warnings about your partner's behavior from people who don't have much authority, from the least important person in the situation? Does an old woman who cleans the flat, and seems to have no reason for a grudge, tell you about your fiancé's hitting his previous girlfriend? Does your son's friend know his family, and say, "Oh, he hits people. He enjoys hitting them." In other words, are they people who see the truth because they have no reason not to, no reason to look at attractive, important appearances, because they play no important part on the stage of the situation? Don't ignore them. The same consideration must be made by people who are trying to help someone they suspect is being abused and psychologically trapped in it.

What it doesn't change is the fact that they are abusers! Because they have the ability to confuse and disguise their personality, their victims have to find a way out of their confusion. Writing down and listing one's grievances, the details of abusive behavior, is a way to help oneself to think clearly, to decide what exactly is wrong, and how serious the situation is.

What kinds of abuse are there, anyway? Counselors and psychologists mention these:

- verbal

- emotional

- psychological

- physical

- sexual

- financial

- spiritual.

You just do not find these kinds of behavior in a loving or even fairly average relationship... None of them is a healthy type of treatment. It is necessary to think about what each of these categories of abuse looks like, and not to be tolerant of any of it. Abused people, victims, become too tolerant too easily. They might say that because they grew up experiencing it, it doesn't shock or affect them as much. The statistics of violence and mental breakdown don't tell that story at all! We also have to be careful of using the word 'normal' badly. 'Normal' means 'in agreement with the norms, rules and guidelines', not 'common'. If fifty-five percent of men beat their wives it wouldn't become 'normal' even though it would be commonplace!

Ask yourself, if you know that you are suffering abuse, what you need to have in a relationship as the bare minimum to live in it. If you decide, and find that after a time you don't get it, then you know you have to leave. Don't keep bending your expectations lower and lower. What would you absolutely love to have in a relationship that would make it happy? Write it down. What is enough to have to make it worthwhile? And what things are absolutely wrong, and cannot be tolerated? Review these definitions. Of course people will have arguments or disagreements... but disagreeing is not the same as having no respect; being angry, not the same as being treated as an object with no rights. Is that what is actually happening? That's abuse. Openness, a good way to handle stress, honesty and fidelity are all things that have to be in a good relationship. You must be conscious of this fact.

People can be too trusting, as well as too suspicious. When a partner is 'love-bombing' another, do we rush to assume that everything said is true, not trying to question it when something seems suspicious? Your list of wishes and your minimum requirements and most important characteristics for a good relationship is obviously very individual. You might be an Antarctic explorer going away for a couple of months every year. It's your passion and part of your job, so having a partner who can accept that and manage without you is a necessity for you. It wouldn't be for most people, but that doesn't make you unreasonable!

Chapter 10
Co-Dependency and Trauma-Bonding

Y ou will hear the word, 'CO-DEPENDENCY' used sometimes by counselors and psychologists as a description of people acting in certain ways. Actually, it's not an official term, but it will help to use that layperson's word to understand this behavior.

It describes one person who invests a lot of energy in regulating, 'rescuing' or helping another person in a specific way, and the person being 'helped' is taking the attention, abusing the giver, and becoming dependent on their help. The helper is also becoming dependent on their role as a 'giver' and is said to be co-dependent with the abuser.

Some people see this behavior as a disease; others as being a logical way of coping in traumatic situations (though obviously it will need to be 'un-learned' in the process of becoming free of trauma bonds). To try to help an abusive person can sound very much like crazy, irrational behavior; at other times co-dependency is treated as a sort of identity which victims cling to. Whether or not it's an identity, it will help you to see clearly and to heal yourself if you just try to understand it. If it's what you are, it may indeed have made some kind of sense at first. Again, don't try to punish yourself!

How does the human brain respond to a threat? There are four basic ways, and it helps to picture a dog to illustrate them.

- FIGHT: imagine the dog with its fur standing on end and its teeth bared! Ready to defend...

- FLIGHT: the dog puts its tail between its legs and runs for its life! This one's too dangerous...

- FREEZE: the dog stops, looks and listens, so that it can decide what it's supposed to do...

- FAWN: the dog rushes up to a stranger, tail wagging, and bends down submissively. Or it rolls over and lets itself be petted and examined.

In this case, 'fawning' is the reaction of someone who is co-dependent. The fawning dog is scared that it's going to be killed or rejected by a stronger, older (if it's a puppy) member of the pack. So it shows that it's useful, co-operative, an ally, a friend... hoping to be allowed to stay in that dog-pack!

In a similar sort of way, someone can try to present himself or herself as being helpful, caring, even like the other person, mimicking them; good to have around. In this way they hope at least to be kept on, maybe even loved.

So a child, too small to fight, too helpless to flee and so unable to decide between these options, fawns in the presence of a cold, abusive, angry or unpredictable parent-figure. Perhaps that parent is also co-dependent in turn, or the other parent is a co-dependent. Either way, the child's brain is going to take up this survival-strategy; it's really not a conscious decision.

The alternative would be to rebel, in other words to fight. As said, this is not always an option for a little child. So little Markie doesn't just become passive in his Mom's presence, but he tries very hard to find out what she wants, to judge her moods, and behave in the way that will, he hopes, get her approval. Children can put a tremendous amount of time into this, and become very good at it! Needless to say, being on his guard all the time will take a huge amount of Markie's energy and peace of mind away. Despite that, you can call him clever: he's a survivor...

When dealing with a narcissistic sociopath, especially a violent one, the same may apply. His or her victim may also be weakened and confused, and it makes sense to adapt rather than fight and risk serious injury. In many cases a narcissist is someone who is dependent on alcohol or drugs, and the way in which these substances affect the moods of this addict is something a victim needs to know. If the victim can help the abuser to reduce or regulate these drugs, or can mitigate their effects, the victim will do it. Little Markie might answer the door when his parents are drunk, to stop the visitor from seeing them; he might hide some of her money from his mother when she's on a binge, and then secretly put it back into her purse when she's sober, knowing what happened when they ran out of money before.

Later in his life, adult Mark is going to have to work to have a normal relationship, because normal relationships are not based on such fear. They're based on trust, and mutual help given by sufficiently independent individuals who can add to their own lives by working together, not rescue. In healthy bonding, as we covered earlier, there is no need to hide oneself from the other: one can be true to oneself. Mark does have to change his mindset, but it's something he has to learn to do gradually. He has to evolve his attitudes and behavior away from the co-dependency and towards maturity so that he can become capable of giving and receiving mutual help. We humans are social animals, like dogs but more so, and by nature we are inter-dependent: neither independent and self-sufficient in isolation, nor inferior, dependent parts joined to serve a group.

What is the exact connection between this co-dependency and trauma-bonding? Simply, when there is a co-dependent pattern, trauma-bonding happens inside the co-dependent relationship. In childhood we need to learn to be attached and loved, before we can become aware of who we are and our relation to other people. It helps us to develop our own personalities and identities, to form our own beliefs about the world. Obviously that can lead to conflict, but it is a part of growing up and being capable of making healthy, adaptive decisions. If you can't tell the difference between what you want and what your significant other wants, you will be handicapped when there are crises, and thrown into chaos when you have to make a decision that other person cannot make for you.

Little Markie, our example, spent so much time second-guessing his parents, especially his mother, that he really had little time to pay attention to himself, so that he could grow up. It sounds rather quaint if you don't think about it: Markie who was so unselfish, so quiet and un-rebellious, Markie who was so easy to look after because he was never any trouble! Deep inside, though, he's had a deprived childhood. He was robbed! Do you see yourself in him? Or someone you know?

Markie never knew safety. When he failed to appease his drunken or suspicious parents and was insulted, neglected or disciplined unfairly, it punished him. When he managed to get some paltry praise out of them, or just got them to leave him in peace for a bit, it was a reward. We've already explained the cycle of double re-enforcement, prize and punishment, in trauma-bonding. We also showed how it tends to degenerate as time goes by, so that there is more punishment and less and less praise - and an almighty addiction in the brain.

The drug he's being hooked on is a mixture of LOVE and FEAR towards a significant other. When adult Mark's girlfriend 'love-bombs' him, he gets feelings of happiness and bonding which are connected to chemicals in the brain, as they should be, but probably more powerfully. Then, for example, when she turns into a screaming tantrum-thrower when he doesn't want them to spend a vacation with her parents, he reacts with intense fear, but also experiences intense loving feelings. These feelings make him think that he's helping her by giving her what she wants, and so he will put his own idea of a holiday aside and agree to her demands, despite knowing that her parents are openly critical of him.

Let us try to understand Mark, then. This is why he says that he can't leave his girlfriend, even though he admits that he's depressed because she's so hard to handle. It's why he feels crazy for still trying to get her parents to like him, even though it's been two years and he's just not succeeding. It's why the memory of what it was like when he met her is so painful, but so beautiful, that he thinks he cannot get anything like that again. He's trying to get his most basic needs fulfilled, as anyone would, but in the wrong way and the wrong place, not being able to see any better way to do it when he was young.

Mark is going to need a lot of love and time to be heard and understood, to grow out of his trauma-bond and co-dependency, and to find his sense of self-worth. He needs to be guided though a process of learning who he really is, of maturing his identity so that he won't confuse his own needs with those of others. Actually, he needs to bond with himself before he can do so with other people. Mark is likely to have a very poor estimate of his worth, and think that he can only find worth in what he does for someone else who has worth. Instead, he could be able to give his own love and personality as a gift to someone else, a precious gift of worth to someone who also has worth.

Mark definitely did NOT deserve to be treated badly as a child, and his counselor must show him that he wasn't abused because of anything he did. He will feel so much better when he realizes that healthy people, or even most victims, don't abuse others. Happy people don't abuse other people! He needs some praise for the way he handled such a hard child-hood, even as he learns to change that way of doing things.

What Mark is going to have to do, of course, is to stop making excuses for other people when they are cruel or selfish to him. Even if his mother and father were themselves children of alcoholics, that doesn't let them off! His girlfriend might have health problems, but why is it that other people have the same problems as she does, yet they don't all start screaming and crying when they can't get what they want? Mark will start to see that someone else's bad behavior is not his fault.

Perhaps female co-dependents are even more likely to see themselves as rescuers. They may accept ill-willed, unattractive people into their lives, perhaps narcissists already weakening and becoming alcoholic and delusional. They can feel so unworthy that they try to earn love from everyone, always giving you gifts, and tense, emotional thanks for offers of help which they always seem to draw, and always refuse. They can seem mature at a very young age, learning to speak politely and to listen long before most other children. Once again, they need to be loved 'without strings' and taught that they can love best when they are loved for who they are, not for what they do. It can be very flattering to be seen as a helper, but such co-dependent helpers are tormenting themselves and not finding the real joy of giving, especially in a rela-tionship.

Chapter 11
Attachment Bonds, Trauma Bonds and Boundaries

A TTACHMENT BONDS have been referred to several times as we are explaining to you how trauma affects people. These are natural links starting between a child and his or her mother and other caregivers, and should form within that child's first two years. They aren't fixed and rigid once formed, and they can change and develop up to and through adult life. Three kinds of attachments exist:

- Secure

- Anxious

- Ambivalent/Avoidant.

Psychologists are observing that SECURE attachment, once attained by the majority of children in the West, is declining to a minority. This is going to be a problem for them in the future. Secure attachment means having a carer, a parent or other person, who is their place of safety as a baby. For example, once a child starts to walk and explore, or to have any kind of unfamiliar experience, she knows that she can run to her mother. If for any reason Mother is out of sight, she learns that she can call her or cry, and that her mother will come and give her safety and love.

Through childhood that figure of attachment will be there as the child's world grows to include all of the house, the area around it, perhaps the houses of family members and friends. Curiosity and attachment can exist in a balance in healthy childhood, so that the child grows up neither as an isolated individual, nor as a passive slave with no desire to leave the primary carer or that person's substitute. When mature we can comfort ourselves, and don't want to be taken over, much as we want companionship and love.

Once securely attached, people can be interdependent, as we described in the previous chapter. They can enjoy not just being loved, but loving someone else. They can exercise self-control, knowing firstly that their desires are not entirely rational and need to be curbed and directed; yet also knowing that they have no reason to fear losing all the good things they desire. Having that lack of fear will enable them to be patient and not impulsive.

ANXIOUS attachment forms when parents or other caregivers are 'helicopter parents'. This means that they are constantly supervising their child or children, even when under the care of others, such as at school. They literally seem to hover over them like a helicopter, hence that use of words. Such children are not allowed to take any responsibility, and have no privacy or autonomy. This kind of style of raising children seems to be on the increase; perhaps a reaction to the increase in society becoming more and more mobile, cosmopolitan, and impersonal, and the sense of danger the media constantly alert us about.

Anxious parents seek to prevent their children from exploring, either forbidding it explicitly or by displaying fear when their child is curious or lost. When such a child is overwhelmed or upset in a situation, for example getting lost in a supermarket, the parent does not so much comfort him or her, but takes away the possibility of that situation recurring. In other words, mother says that from now on her child must stay with her when she does the shopping, by staying seated in the shopping trolley or cart, and never leave her sight.

What happens if you grew up like this? You may think of the world as a place without any safety at all... Of course there is danger in the world, but every day most people manage to go about their business, to learn new things, to travel and to live without being attacked. Such people don't see this. All failure is thought of as being a catastrophe! You don't learn from mistakes, they seem to believe, repeating the oft-heard refrain: "It must never happen again."

AMBIVALENT attachment can be described in the following way. The care-giver is inconsistent. At times she, or he, is aware of the child and pays attention. At other times that presence or awareness is taken away. The child might be treated as lovable on one occasion, and as irritating on another. Sometimes the child has love, sometimes not. It swings back and forth.

Such a person will try not to be dependent, but will not know how to be independent... They will not have any sense of peace within, and instead will feel chaos. Danger will seem no less unpleasant than the normal chaos of their lives, so perhaps they will tend to take risks. Strangely, when it is calm and ordered in their surroundings, they will feel very uncomfortable, and hate looking inward - avoiding introspection. Such styles of attachment also seem to be increasing in Western society, and perhaps in other cultures too.

Trauma-bonding relates to an attachment style where the person a child-victim is attaching to does harm but prevents that victim from re-covering by himself or herself, or with the help of other people and cir-cumstances. Instead, the victim is not allowed to admit that he or she has feelings of fear, for example. Such children learn that they have to 'bottle up' their emotions, and are not allowed to question why they are being punished. They will feel numbed as they learn to do what they are commanded to, sensing a disconnection between actions and feelings. A powerful negative emotion they are often taught is shame, especially for their failures, and their failures to hide their feelings!
Growing up in this way, they will feel that if they try to distance them-selves from their abusive caregiver, they'll be in trouble. If they experi-ence their own emotions or display them, they'll also be in trouble! So they become dependent on their abuser, yet with fear instead of trust. If they are separated from them, as we have already seen before, they will feel desolated and depressed. If they'd been allowed to distance themselves enough to see their situation, then the truth of what is hap-pening would have been obvious. But they are being trapped, usually deliberately... These children are at the time of life when our con-sciences, our senses of right and wrong, are developing. Shame is a

powerful feeling in a child, and when that child is made to feel ashamed of everything he or she does or thinks, then it becomes a habit.

The response to these feelings of shame cannot be 'fight or flight' as it was explained in the previous chapter. The child has been conditioned powerfully to believe that he or she may not leave - flee; and is also shamed for being angry - fighting. Thus, the pleasing, fawning reaction is the only way out, as has been established.

Shamed, traumatized children haven't been disciplined at all - they have no idea of what is really wrong about what they have done, or how to know right from wrong. It's just a case of pleasing the whims of their caregiver! There is no consistency in their punishments, no increase in severity for more serious wrongdoings. They have no idea of the boundaries of behavior.
The boundaries of behavior are very important, and a traumatized child is going to find it very hard to set them. Boundaries relate to our WANTS and to our NEEDS: and to the difference between them. The abusive, toxic parent is someone who hardly sees the difference in their own life; and their child or children, made to be dependent on their whims and moods, are made slaves to their wants, wants treated as if they were needs. As we know, the alcoholic living in misery on the street needs a shelter and a home, and decent food. Yet he's begging for money, and using most of it to buy more alcohol. We can see, if we look at the situation, that his needs and wants are not the same, even if they should be.

An abuser who has made someone dependent on them has made that victim so attuned to the abuser's wants that it is hard for the victim, trying to break free of the bond, to see the abuser's needs as distinct from their wants. Maybe, grown up, the victim runs around trying to be helpful to everyone, especially to family members, who take all of her ministering to their needs and demand more, so that she drains herself to the point of exhaustion. Are you doing this? Is anyone you know, like this?She needs to see that they are blind to her need for time and space, or her responsibilities towards others again. She doesn't have to be a slave to their wants, because they need to learn how to be responsible, or to be less selfish - but she hasn't let them. She needs to learn, as she heals, to see what they need, and what she herself needs. Other people who are recovering from trauma bonds in childhood may fall into the trap of trying to help the poor, the needy, the far-off, so much that they neglect their primary relationships, their spouses and children, for example. Deep inside, they may feel driven to be rescuers because of the deep sense of shame bashed into them from their youth, the shame already mentioned. This is not to condemn them; instead, it is to point out that they are acting out of an anxious or ambivalent feeling, lacking the peace of a secure attachment in their lives. When they have that, they will be able to act out of love rather than fear (which is at the root of their shame and their hyperactivity) and to see their priorities so much more easily.

Chapter 12
Trauma and the Brain

N ow it is time to take a walk through the human brain and understand why it behaves as it does - why YOU and I behave as we do!

So much of what we are explaining to you in this book relates to understanding yourself and realizing why you have behaved as you did, and in following chapters, how you can recover from your experiences of trauma and being in a trauma bond. It helps so much to understand the human brain. Then after looking at a few more themes in trauma, we will dedicate the rest of the book to helpful advice and strategies for healing.

The first thing about the brain is to understand that not only are there two similar halves working in tandem, but that there are two separate types of brain!

Look at any good picture of the human brain. In front, above and to the sides are the folded, wavy structures we think of instantly when someone says the word, 'brain'. This is called the CEREBRAL CORTEX, if you want to know. The cortex deals with memory, reasoning, calculating; and seeing, hearing, feeling from a conscious point of view. It's what you are reading or listening with now; it's what you are aware with. Our personality, the choices we make and our individual consciousness have their physical element here.

This is where information our brain seeks in the senses and finds with our eyes, ears and so on, is processed. Our ability to do all the things animals struggle to do, or can't do at all, comes in the main from our very large and ordered brain cortex. Our reason is our greatest tool, more than all the teeth and fur and flippers and shells and rapid movement, or great size and strength, of different animals which use these things to survive.

Underneath the cortex is the rest of the brain: the CEREBELLUM at the back, which deals with your movement and co-ordination; the BRAIN STEM which unites all the regions of the brain, the spinal cord going forth to all your nerves, and several other parts it isn't necessary to go into now. These parts of the brain deal with all the functions we have in common with animals: eating, sleeping, sheltering, mating, nurturing, fighting, fleeing... We have a cortex, but this doesn't deny the role of the rest of our brain. To be human is not to be totally 'un-animal', but to be 'animal' lifted up into something higher by another part of us that is not just physical. The animal functions, meanwhile, carry on all the time, and more than any animal, we are conscious of them. However, they run by themselves normally, our control over them being limited and sporadic.

Both types of brain influence our behavior. Stress, as we are considering in relation to trauma, is not a thought - in the cortex - as much as a reaction - in the brain stem or "ANIMAL BRAIN" as we can call it. This part of our brains keeps us breathing, digesting, standing or walking, without having to do it consciously all the time. So, for example, we can hear the words, "Breathe deeply!" and make a conscious effort to do so. However, breathing will carry on, calmly for most of the time, without our being aware of or directing it. This is the reason that we don't die in our sleep every time we go to bed. If we are choking or taking in gas instead of air, however, powerful instincts from the animal brain take over and make us conscious of the need to get fresh air, so that this part of the brain is in charge until the danger has passed.

The 'fight', 'flight', 'freeze' or 'fawn' reactions are all reactions of the animal brain. Anyone in a life-threatening situation such as a war, an attack by a wild animal, an accident, or any one of a great many situations we all know of, has to deal with these powerful and life-preserving instincts. However, they can strain our bodies and affect our brain-cortexes, as we can all testify to.

One of the most important differences between the cortex and the rest of the brain is that our reason acts more slowly than our animal reactions. This is part of why, as mentioned, we have a lot of control over our reason, but less over our instincts from moment to moment. Take this example: if you are driving at night in a car or other automobile, your reason has made you aware of the speed of the vehicle and the direction you're driving in. These are your choices. Suddenly, an owl that was trying to fly across the road, but was blinded and confused by the bright lights of the traffic, gets thrown across the glass of your front windscreen and trapped there by the force of the air. You have such a fright that you slam on the brakes! Realizing in the next couple of seconds that the car is skidding now, and that the windscreen isn't broken, you take your foot off the brake and try to regain control of the car's movement, as it slows down more gradually. By the time the owl struggles and manages to slide off the glass, and regains its instincts to be able to fly again, you are beginning to be fully conscious of what has happened, are using the word, 'owl' in your cortex, and are aware that the car is no longer out of control. And once the owl has landed on a fence, still in shock but able to tend to its bruises and its disordered flight feathers, you are driving along somewhat faster again; still in shock but aware of what caused your reaction, what that over-reaction caused the car to do, what could have happened if it had skidded off the road and crashed into the trees and fences alongside the highway, how you managed to keep it on the road and stop skidding, and telling the story to your memory in words and pictures.

In this example we can see the speed and power of a driver's animal reaction to a sudden movement and obstruction of his eyes. His cortex, his reason, takes longer to work, and has to act against his instincts, forcing him to lift his foot from the brake pedal. Even his awareness of his balance being out of control, of the noise of screeching tires, came to him before his reason decided to intervene and change his protective behavior.

So, having been so much faster than your reason in this example, your animal brain will also go back to normal more slowly than your cortex. Once you arrive at your hotel, you'll still be in a state of mild shock. Probably you'll decide to drink a glass of whisky before eating your supper. You may have an unpleasant dream that night!

How does that relate to trauma? This example was a one-off; but the effect lasted. How much more, for example, a soldier who has to face danger in war during months, or on and off over years? The constant level of arousal and fear that soldier experiences will not just go away once the war ends. Likewise, being in a situation of 'danger' as the brain sees it, in an abusive relationship (in fact, some abusive relationships are dangerous, quite literally) over time, will have a long-lasting effect on all of our brain. The animal brain cannot be switched off instantly once the reason knows its job
is done.

Returning soldiers may find themselves blazing with sudden anger at relatively small accidents or incidents. They have been accustomed to being in survival mode, to needing their 'fight' reaction at any moment to defend themselves and others. Now they need to see things from the point of view of reason, take it more slowly. Yet the animal part of their brain is still hyper-stimulated, and it reacts, in any case, very quickly. What about having a violent, abusive childhood? Perhaps anger and fear were being stirred up constantly in you. You became used to living with sudden episodes of anger. Years later, when under stress in a rela-tionship of love or of work, that anger, modeled by an abusive parent, may well up in you, out of proportion to the injustice done. Your reason tells you that the past is dead and gone, that your present is different, but your animal brain has been conditioned to react without intelligent control, and acts as it 'remembers'. You may shock yourself by your re-action. This is not to justify acting by impulse - but now you can see why you do, as a step to restoring a healthy mind.

When you are traumatized by an abusive partner, it can affect your memory and increase your irritability. No - it's not early senility. Your memory is being disrupted by your being hyper-aware, seeking to flee when it is possible, or to fawn and please that unpredictable person. You simply cannot concentrate as you would do if you could be calm. Your animal brain is too busy taking attention away from your thinking brain. Your reason tells you that you should be able to remember some incident well; but it needs to be considerate! This is not your fault. Your reason might tell you that it will be less stressful for you, and easier to control your abuser, if you don't snap at him or her. Yet you find yourself doing it again and again! Once again, in a stressed, hyper-aroused state, your animal brain is trying to protect you, and it makes you defend yourself verbally before your rational brain can think that the best form of defense might be silence.

People who have a different experience and end up being seriously controlled and crushed inwardly by a narcissistic abuser may not experience such strong, manifested aggression. They might seem passive, but even if that is you, you would feel strong, non-verbal feelings of fear or arousal that have been re-enforced in you over time (in childhood, maybe) and again during the course of that relationship. If, let us say, you were able to leave that abusive person and find a place of safety, what we have understood about your double brain will explain why you would be aware that you are out of danger, physically, but that you still cannot sleep properly, and keep on waking suddenly with fear of being attacked. Sleep is controlled not by reason, but by instinct.

This is why some doctors and psychiatrists prescribe medication to those who suffer from trauma and depression. To seek that help and get it, is to understand that there is a connection between your brain and your body. Medical advice cannot be given here, as to whether medication would benefit you. It is enough to say to you that you have to look after both parts of your brain, and look after your body, to recover well from trauma and trauma-bonding. Recovery will involve all of them, and a pill can't do that on its own. Understanding how you are put together is a great help to managing your life!

Yes, it's complicated! Your brain is probably the most complex thing in the universe. Galaxies are so much vaster, but they are nearly all made up of stars. Stars, stars and more stars; planets and more planets... dust and gas. That's it, folks! Your brain is made of complex chemicals, structures, connections, all joined to your complex body. Never mind your complex thoughts! Never mind that your thinking jumps from the physical to everything you are conscious of, thus transcending matter itself! You're complicated, but you're worth it... So be gentle on yourself in recovery. Just be aware that it will take thought and decisions, practice and time, physical exercise and care. These are all the kind of things we humans are made to do, anyway.

We are not perfect, and our brains, hormones and bodies can work badly in trauma. However, if we remember that we can literally see our thoughts, then we have a way to control ourselves better. We don't just think: we can analyze what we think.

Stress makes all kinds of conditions worse, triggers headaches and indigestion, and so on. When your animal brain is constantly being aroused and disturbed by a toxic relationship instead of just at a few sudden moments in the jungle, it will affect your body in the long-term. That stress isn't a symptom of an abnormal brain - it's a sign that your brain and body are reacting as expected to an abnormal situation. Treating the effects of stress will be by doing exercises such as stretching, breathing practice, disciplining your sleep; and taking part in relaxing activities such as yoga, prayer and meditation, to focus the mind; even sauna treatment and special diets can help. More will be said of these later.

Chapter 13
Cognitive Dissonance and Trauma-Bonding

P sychologists use the words COGNITIVE DISSONANCE to describe the stress that people may experience when their actions and their beliefs do not align, and can refer also to the stress we feel when some of our beliefs do not seem to be in agreement with one another. For example, Mrs. Pettinfluff may be very fond of all kinds of animals; however, she also likes and eats steak and roast chicken. She is aware of what could be a contradiction, and it is quite upsetting. Unless she can find a logical way to justify both, she might be swayed to rationalize it, perhaps by saying, "I never knew the cows and bulls and cocks and hens I eat when they were alive, so I don't have to feel upset if I eat them." Otherwise, she could try to bias her confirmation of the conflict by avoiding evidence: for example, if there is an article claiming that farm animals feel a lot of distress and pain, she will refuse to read it. Or, for another example, she could actually avoid the chapter in a book of spiritual advice where the author says that people shouldn't give the love that is meant for other human beings to animals; because to accept what it says, regarding the other side of it, would mean that she's irrational when she feels affection for animals.

A victim of abuse suffers all kinds of cognitive dissonance when, for example, she believes that she loves and needs her abuser. At the same time he is treating her very badly, and she also believes that he is going to harm her by burning her in the fire. How can she love him when she believes that such cruelty is a possibility?

In trauma-bonding, a victim will experience a lot of cognitive dissonance during the cycle of abuse and reconciliation. The repetition of this cycle, and the compulsion she might feel to persevere with her abuser, clash with one another. "It keeps on happening that he hits me," she may say to herself, "but I feel so strongly that I can make him see why he's taking drugs, and get him to stop." It has been said that a victim who leaves an abuser in a relationship usually comes back, on average seven times!

When we are seriously caught up in a contradiction, a cognitive dissonance, we often react with denial. It's probably the simplest way to avoid conflict. We are left feeling free, in a somewhat frantic way, to imagine that everything is actually all right, or to hope that in the future this person will be better. In the moment of abuse or the middle of neglect, it can help a victim to live another day, you could say; but after living with it for a long time, it will be an obstacle to making any kind of calm judgment or accepting reality.

Once again it has to be spelled out what abusers are doing to their victims, and how. It is a sort of mental hostage-taking; we have seen that Stockholm Syndrome is a similar survival-strategy. There is a perceived danger or threat to the victim's life and integrity (physical or psychological), a menace to their personality (victims feel de-personalized); then he or she gets treatment that looks to be kindness and love, but is just the bait covering the hook of hostile, critical, uncaring behavior that always follows.

Abusers isolate their victims. That could be by trying to force them to stay at home, or for example, even by moving with her to a new city where she doesn't know anyone. Some of them will convince their victims that they don't need a mobile 'phone, or to have a connection to the internet! More subtly, abusers might try to discourage victims from contacting friends and family. This could be by showing rude, critical and dismissive behavior to everyone in front of a husband, let us say, when a couple is visiting his family together. The family members may react angrily, but in this case the abusive wife doesn't care, because she knows that it will put them off giving future invitations to visit. Then when her husband intends to see them on his own, she might suggest syrupily that they should rather go out for a drive to the country, or might try to make him feel bad that he would dare to leave her alone! Abusers may try to make their victims doubt that friends and family care about them, accusing them of strategies and secrecy (the abuser's very own strategies!!). This is to make them see reality as they want them to, and to break them away from the validation and objectivity of other people's viewpoints.

Once they have isolated their victims, abusers try to make victims believe that they have nowhere else to go to. They appeal to victims' senses of loyalty and to promises made, even as they are busy betraying them. (How many narcissists are faithful spouses? Very few.) Here we can make a point that typical narcissists have absolutely no loyalty to promises, not the slightest intention of abiding by them. To a narcissist, such would be a weakness. A promise is simply a means to get something out of someone, a trap, a disguise, a way to make a (false) impression. This has relevance to seeking divorce and financial freedom from one of these people. In a book it isn't possible to judge all cases, but it's enough to say that a marriage-ceremony with a narcissist, who lies so much and whose intentions are so toxic, is not likely to be valid. From a victim's point as well, there is likely to be such a lack of knowing the real abuser, or if the abuse has started already, such a lot of confusion and fear, that you couldn't call the promise free, knowing and willing. There is a lot to think about on this issue.

Cognitive dissonance in a seriously-abused victim will have that person swinging between two opposing ideas, thinking one thing in one minute, and the opposite the next. Beautiful fantasies of getting 'love-bombed' clash with ugly realizations of abuse and lack of love. These realizations are not very pleasant and offer serious challenges, so that denial becomes very tempting.

PART TWO - RESOLVING DISSONANCE AND BREAKING TRAUMA BONDS

Breaking a trauma bond can only happen when cognitive dissonance has been resolved first. This is important to realize. To get out of cognitive dissonance, a victim will need to do the following:

- To face the truth relentlessly. Many counselors ask their clients to write a list of every hateful, abusive or unpleasant deed their partner has done, and when, and how often. They must read it every time they feel like returning, or dreaming about their romantic first encounters...

- To keep repeating that they are not to blame. When someone accepts this, it will act against the irrational hope that a victim can help, save or change his or her abuser, or has any obligation to try to do it. Even if the abuser wanted the victim to accept blame, that is not a reason to believe it!

- To call the abuser, an 'abuser'. A victim must lose any sense of false shame in referring to their abuser by a word with negative meaning, such as narcissist, unfaithful, or sociopath. Exact definitions aren't what's needed here: you have to call the pattern of abuse an abuse, to understand and come to terms with it; and the guilty party, guilty, to realize what that person has done. This isn't being judgmental, but rather having sound judgment!

- To talk about his or her abuse to people who will listen and sympathize, and are going to understand. In the same way, anyone who refuses to accept that it's abuse, or is offended by talk of the subject, must be avoided. Join a victims' group! These people are people for whom the TRUTH matters, and they've been where you are, so they will be good for you, when you are trying to understand the truth about yourself.

Sometimes abused people have a sort of breakthrough while still in the toxic relationship, a sort of epiphany where they suddenly see the truth, lose their cognitive dissonance, and see once and for all that they have to get out. If that is you, you will know. If that isn't what you've had... don't wait for one! If you plan to get out and are seeking help, then take heart from the fact that most people making the actual move are still feeling very confused, and only solve their cognitive dissonance some time after leaving their abuser. People resolve their seesawing thoughts when they can open up and see outside themselves to objective reality.

In the first stages of counseling it is quite good to look at outside reality, to situate yourself in the truth and to calm your inner conflicts, especially the dissonance. In later stages of becoming free of the trauma bonds, then you will need to look inside yourself and your memories, to experience growth and healing. Those stages are where you will learn to take responsibility for your life, and how to make good decisions. This is 'empowering' and not at all like blaming yourself or feeling shame.

Looking within one's history of trauma will take you back to identifying who your abusers were in childhood, or if not quite abusers, which caregivers at least neglected you or treated you with ambivalence or coldness. You will see what your needs were, and in what way your caregivers failed to meet them, and how that affected you.

Deeper personal growth happens to someone who suffered abuse when, let us say, she no longer refers to herself as a "victim". This isn't denial, let it be emphasized. You see, to get lots of sympathy from others who listen to you, and to enjoy that too much, is to be blind to the much greater peace and enjoyment of life that results from being in a healthy and normal state of mind. It's actually narcissistic! That was said to be shocking, but by definition it is so. It is a case of thinking the way your narcissistic abuser thought of himself or herself! It's what the abuser wanted you to identify with, so that you could understand and feel his or her every flight of emotion, anticipate every selfish desire. It is a tragedy indeed when some victims stay in this stage for years, even the rest of their lives.

There's an additional reason for not wanting to stay stuck in the stage of identifying as a victim: such a person is likely to find another sociopath and maybe get involved in a relationship with them. Even an abuser whose personality is more hidden and subtle? It has been pointed out that someone who is happy and confident, at peace, will not be drawn to abusive personalities, even if those narcissists try to be charming. If they've been there before, and understood what deceived them, they'll recognize it and feel it as being unpleasant and false.

A 'survivor' of abuse is someone who looks after herself. She will be able to find her deep inner wounds and heal them because it won't cause her shame to see them; she won't feel shame, because she will have realized and believed that the trauma wasn't her fault. She can see that taking responsibility from now on is not built on feeling guilty for the past, but on looking to the future with realism and being at peace. All of this will be hard but worthwhile work.

If you are the reader who is reading this to try to help and understand someone else, you will be able to glean some important bits of advice from these considerations. First of all, you can be the sympathetic listener who can provide objectivity and confirmation to the victim that they have indeed been abused, that their decision to leave the abusing partner was necessary, and who can calm them down so that they can begin to get over their cognitive dissonance.

You will call the abuser an abuser, and encourage the victim to do the same. Never let the victim say that the abuse happened to them because it was their fault; remind them that there is no need to feel shame at all. They are not to take any blame. They, too, must make a list of all the crimes and abuses they know that the victim has suffered, and try to question them gently but carefully to find out what other things happened that they don't know about already. Then, further down the road to recovery, you will stop treating that person as a victim, and call them a survivor, respecting their ability to take responsibility for themselves, and their need to be less dependent on you than they were at the beginning, when they began to trust you and had to see things from your point of view.

Looking at what abusers do to their victims will possibly explain to you, as an outsider trying to help a loved one, why you might encounter resistance and denial, or suspicion, from that loved one. We mentioned denial; the easiest way to avoid the pain of knowing that something is wrong and that he or she is living in the midst of it. A stage closer to acceptance of reality would be when a victim is panicky and uncertain, admitting that things are wrong but that he or she is confused as to how, and feeling that it is safer to go on as things have been, than try to change. So if you have to insist on getting the facts right for the victim, do it gently.

Being bonded to an abuser seems crazy, but as we saw in our chapter on the brain, the bonding in trauma is not coming from the rational brain, but rather the animal brain, trying to survive. Victims, you are NOT stupid! You are not uneducated. A feature of all kinds of abuse, whether you think of religious cults, political extremism or terrorism, or the personal and individual damage that happens in families, in work, and in what should be love-relationships - is that victims can be of average or above-average intelligence. Even psychologists can become abused.

Breaking cognitive dissonance, as said, will happen more quickly than breaking the trauma-bond. The deeper freedom that comes from not being bound will mean that survivors will understand how they used to try desperately to please everyone, to sacrifice themselves in a harmful way, to abandon themselves, how they were co-dependent. Finally, in the process of healing and growing personally, people who were traumatized will become not just 'survivors' but 'thrivers' because they will have confronted that 'false self' they grew up with. This important confrontation and the transformation that results usually needs another person or people to make it happen. Those people will not be clung to by the person growing out of abuse, in their old, dependent way, because after personal growth the former victim will be able to take responsibility for life and not let himself or herself be directed passively by other people.

The person who acts as a catalyst usually causes a feeling that takes you back to your childhood, reminding you of your deepest wound from that time. Whether or not you were raised by a narcissist, the sudden crisis you will experience is really an opportunity to be healed. You will have a choice to be the 'real you' instead of the person you thought you had to be. You will not have to do this out of fear, but because of the truth. Any compulsive types of behavior you used to indulge in to kill a deep sense of helplessness will lose their hold on you, and your sense of shame will wither away. Shame that results from abuse is not your shame; it just makes you sick, makes you feel unworthy. Breaking the trauma bond is to accept yourself, and when it is done, you will feel at peace, even a little too quiet on the inside, just because you were so used to trauma.

The 'walk' of your life will bring a few challenges in the final stages of freedom. A victim will need to break contact with his or her abuser, very importantly; and also mentally, with places and people who were part of that trauma-bond. You don't want to be tempted to keep on thinking of yourself as a victim.

Have you really got out of that trauma bond? When 'love-bombing' looks shallow and nauseating, when you don't keep hoping that your abuser will change, when you never try to excuse your abuser's behavior, not even in your own thoughts, and are no longer living in fear of that toxic person; when you don't help people who also hurt you during the time of your abuse, out of guilt or felt obligation towards them, don't keep on trying to convince abusive people by explaining why their actions were wrong, when they won't accept responsibility; when you have no attraction to other, new people who are abusive, so familiar to you now... then you can say that it's broken.

You will also need to break any trauma-bonding with your original abuser, normally a member of your family. Breaking that first-ever bond should make any others you still feel, to break as well. It is true that some sufferers didn't grow up in a trauma-bond. They will have fallen as adults into a trap of a relationship with someone whose inner wounds are the same or similar. Perhaps insecurity or rejection haunt this person, and that person must have been abusive in some way, out of that need, for a trauma-bond to form.

In the future...? You cannot blame yourself for all sorts of people being attracted to you, since there are all types in the world; but you must ask yourself whom you are going to choose to make a part of your life. The moment anyone in your life reveals signs of being a manipulative character (and manipulators can hide for a while), you will not tolerate their behavior, and you won't start thinking it's your job to teach them to be caring and honest!

If people you have known all along while you were being abused keep reminding you of how silly you were, as they think, how wrong to have tolerated what you did - and they are doing this out of a kind of desire to help you, but full of negativity, stay away from them! Some people actually enjoy opining like this out of a sense of superiority over you. That's not love...

Chapter 14
PTSD and Traumatic Experiences

T he abbreviation 'PTSD' stands for 'Post-Traumatic Stress Disorder'. This refers to symptoms experienced after a terrifying or unpleasant happening, sometimes for years after, at other times much less. Victims experience powerful memories or 'flashbacks', recurring dreams, and sudden bursts of anger, fear or sadness. They will seek to avoid whatever is associated with them.

The most common use of the term PTSD is in the case of military personnel who return to civilian life, or perhaps from war to peacetime service, and experience mental distress because of what they experienced in combat.

There are different kinds of PTSD. NORMAL PTSD is a response to a sudden stress that any healthy person might experience, from an event that disrupts their entire life. This could be a car-accident, a robbery, a burst appendix requiring emergency surgery, and so on. They may feel numb and disconnected from their emotions, cut off from reality, or the opposite: too emotional. This reaction does not last more than a few weeks in most cases, and recovery is usually spontaneous.

CO-MORBID PTSD is when a sufferer has another problem together with a trauma. This could be depression, addiction to drugs, phobias, etc. Feelings of guilt and failure might be adding to the after-shock, a case seen in soldiers who witnessed death, or had to kill in battle or defense. Such sufferers will need treatment of the other condition or conditions as well.

ACUTE PTSD happens because of a sudden shock involving a loss. For example, losing a loved one from a sudden heart-attack, or having your house flattened by an earthquake. People in such cases often benefit from leaving the scene of the trauma for a time, to recover elsewhere.

So-called UNCOMPLICATED PTSD is when the victim experiences a sudden once-off trauma, but later, over a significant period, keeps "reliving" the traumatic events. They will tend to avoid anything associated with the trauma or reminding them of it. A good example of this is a rape victim. She may try to avoid all adult men. Or, being married, she will find sex with her husband impossibly stressful because it constantly reminds her of her traumatic experience of forced sex with a stranger.

COMPLEX PTSD is also called "Extreme Stress Disorder" and refers to a shock, injury, trauma, that happens repeatedly over a long period. Childhood abuse of any type is one of the most obvious examples. They may also have other psychological problems caused by these experiences, and yet they are often labeled or misdiagnosed as being anti-social, bipolar, and so on. Because they were traumatized over a long period, they may need a longer time to heal.

Now, quite clearly, a traumatic childhood - or an abusive relationship in adulthood with a narcissistic personality - will cause the latter type of PTSD, i.e. complex PTSD symptoms. What is the relevance of this to trauma-bonding? It's the simple fact of abuse being a trauma. In the case of bonding unhealthily during a cycle of abuse in a relationship over a long time, and later being able to leave that relationship, the victim will, nevertheless, have to come to terms with after-effects. Victims don't, as we have explained, just suddenly get over it!

Victims of complex PTSD can sometimes try to escape their feelings by overeating, binge-drinking, drug- or medication-overuse, pornography, gambling and so on. Dear reader, up until now we haven't mentioned some of the things victims do to try to dull their guilt or confusion, their substitute addictions for their emotional, "brain-addictions" trauma sucked them into. This escapist behavior can show itself either during an abusive relationship, or especially after it's over, when the withdrawal symptoms from victims' habitual over-arousal and constant fear cause them to crave some kind of excitement or comfort. Is that what you feel forced to do? Are you stuck, it seems, in another cycle of excitement, shame and boredom? Don't feel ashamed! Of course these things aren't good for you, which you know anyway, but we must repeat to you that it is a reaction by your animal brain to situations you couldn't control. You need to stop worrying, and to realize that your abuse has made you confused and guilty. Once you see that you can and should stop feeling responsible for your abuse, and have taken control of your life by getting away from a toxic relationship, you will actually be healing the inner pain that causes you to want to run away from it all... Other people who care can help; sharing your life-story can make you feel greater peace.

Let us look at PTSD in detail. What exactly is happening? The victim suffers from vivid, intrusive memories, nightmares and sudden overwhelming emotions. These cause immediate biological arousal - your heart rate goes up, stress-hormones are released, things like digestion are put on pause... and the extreme arousal is so unpleasant that you try to avoid whatever triggers these reactions. That is understandable: your animal-brain is trying to protect you. However, that stops your reasoning-brain from working on and resolving the conflict. The emotions become stuck in a sort of cycle (rather like the cycle of abuse), a kind of loop.

We need to process our emotions, and recognize patterns in our experiences, in order to control our lives and behavior. This is the way we are, and the way we should be. In order to protect our lives, we need safety - and safety, psychology shows us, is being able to predict things. When everything seems chaotic, we can't do that.

Sudden crises, or experiences cut off from the rest of our lives, emotionally different, intense and confusing, can't be classified and made predictable. That is exactly what an abuser was trying to do, to cut his or her victim's support off, so as to control that victim, to CREATE chaos! Many stressful experiences are familiar or understandable, and so won't provoke PTSD. Yet sudden life-threatening events are possibly the only really brand-new, uncontrollable experiences we have in later childhood or adulthood. This chaos destroys the kind of necessary, natural assumptions we make about the world around us.

TREATING P.T.S.D. AND HOW IT COULD HELP THE ABUSED

In the case of PTSD, there are some specific therapies which are proving to help sufferers, such as returning military personnel. Would those help you, recovering from a toxic relationship? We believe that they could. Let us describe what they are like...

Some therapists are using exposure therapy to help victims. This involves presenting them with visual triggers, or remembering-exercises, to get them to experience their unpleasant memories again, but in safe, supporting and knowledgeable surroundings. They have someone with them for them to express what they feel, share what they remember, and to think about how it makes them want to act. This simply allows their minds to order, understand and accept what happened - and this stops the cycle of avoidance and reminding. Victims will need positive re-enforcement and encouragement, and to be taught how to relax physically while re-living their memories. Medical monitors can confirm that their hearts are starting not to beat so fast, their blood-pressure not rising so much, and so on.

Victims may indeed need other treatment, as will be the case of long-term narcissistic abuse. However, this PTSD-based approach could be used, for example, when someone has written a list of all the things she suffered over several years. She could remember the times when she was locked in a room by her abusive boyfriend for 'spending too much money' or 'not being there when he returned from work'. Such remembering of those exact conditions is going to be stressful, but with a compassionate and understanding counselor, and a support-group, she can actually confirm and accept what happened, and neither avoid it, nor re-live the terror and abandonment she felt alone. It can help her to realize that she needs to stay away from him, but that each time she becomes less emotional about sharing her memories, and labels her abuse as abuse, she is breaking away from the hold he used to have on her. Working over memories will help a recovering survivor to have less fear of them, and in that way, should help her, or him, to experience fewer recurring, unpleasant dreams.

Role-playing might help a victim to be prepared to communicate calmly and firmly with her abuser's family members, if this becomes legally necessary; to expose herself in her mind to what she will say to them, and how she will handle her feelings. These are all cognitive approaches; to manage your feelings by understanding them, and guiding them firmly but gently to a resolution to accept reality without fear or shame. It could help a victim of sexual abuse to communicate with a new romantic partner, to be without shame or fear of intimacy, or to explain what the new person will have to accept and be patient about.

Recovering victims may have to handle explosive feelings of anger once they start to accept that they were abused. These may be inappropriate, or directed at people who have nothing to do with their trauma bonds. If so, therapy can explain to them that they are stressed, that stress makes concentrating and tolerating distraction harder, and that their animal brains are trying to protect them, but in the wrong way. It will also re-assure them that it is not their fault, and that those who share their lives will benefit from understanding this, too. They must not take such anger personally.

IMPORTANT EMOTIONAL AND MENTAL TECHNIQUES TO HELP P.T.S.D. SUFFERERS AND ABUSE-VICTIMS

Now it's time to look at some important emotional and mental techniques to help you to recover. Most of them have been developed for treating "shell-shocked" soldiers who were and are being badly affected in war and other combat situations; they are no less effective when modified for anyone who has been in an abusive relationship. This is whether abused as a child, or as an adult.

Something to understand, before we begin, is the idea we call THE FACT OF YOUR FEELINGS. The following example describes what the fact of your feelings is: the man who thinks he's a cabbage. This unfortunate individual has a strong, unwanted, irrational but very powerful feeling, and an idea in his mind that goes with it, that he is not a man at all, but a cabbage! No mockery is intended here: victims of psychopathic conditions may hallucinate or suffer strange delusions which they cannot help. The poor man is, as a result, terrified of white butterflies. Why? Because, he reasons, they'll lay their eggs on him; then those eggs will hatch into caterpillars. You and I know, and in most cases he will be aware, that it's not a FACT that he's a CABBAGE, or that caterpillars will eat him alive... but it is a FACT, that he has a strong, persistent FEELING that he is a cabbage. Medication may suppress the feeling in this case of a disturbed mind, but counseling would get him to open up and look at just exactly what he is feeling. He needs to look at it, not avoid it, to get better.

In any case - the fact of your feeling helpless, frustrated, that there is no way out; that your abuser is going the wrong way, tragically, but he or she seems so lovable... is a feeling. You will need to be precise about your inner sensations, learn to say if they are, for example, relief mixed with despair, or happiness mixed with silliness, or heart-wrenching pain mixed with an overpowering love and a wee bit of anger... or whatever your feelings are, dear reader. We men tend to over-simplify them in an attempt to control them. That simply won't work in this situation. You might say, "I'm angry."
A therapist might ask, "How are you angry? Talk more about it and tell me in what way."
"I said. I'm angry. Period."
"From what you told me, as to why you're here: you are in a rage, you feel that you've been done a great injustice and then ignored, you feel hate towards any authority figure because you feel their cold lack of care."
"Yeah. That's true."
"So, you're not just 'angry'; there's a lot more in your feelings! Do you see what I mean?"

Other people, perhaps acquaintances and family members, try a sort of "idiot's logic" on you. To quote the first example, if you have these dreadful irrational feelings of being a cabbage, they'd say, "But you're not a cabbage. That's not logical. You know that. So why do you tell yourself that you are?" They missed the whole point: you don't know why, and they don't have a clue, either.

When you understand that you have an animal brain and a reasoning brain, it begins to become clear. Something in your animal brain is trying to protect you, and the process has gone wrong. However, your animal brain has its function in your life, and you couldn't live without it. You have to manage it sometimes with your reasoning brain, your cerebral cortex. If you were to identify WHEN you get these thoughts, and WHAT you feel exactly, you can begin to find out what's wrong, what the trauma was - because it's an animal brain's response to trauma. Then, you need to do mental exercises regularly to confront what you feel, remind yourself of the truth (without any sense of guilt or shame), and calm yourself.

The word, 'disassociation' is used to define what many of us do when asked to say what our feelings were, for example when keeping a diary. We may say what we thought, describe what we did, but not express what we FELT during these events or when having these thoughts. We have, so to speak, disassociated our feelings from the rest of our minds. Emotional awareness consists of being able to describe and understand what our feelings are, to confront them, and so to be more aware of, more able to manage, our animal brains.

Now we shall look at some techniques to handle flashbacks, emotional avoidance, and disassociation.

A word here about 'managing' our emotions: it isn't possible, nor would it be healthy, to force, stop, or wipe out our emotions or thoughts, in a sort of instant obedience. Instead, we manage them by allowing them to run about within certain limits (something like a dog in the park), and when they stray, we encourage them to operate in the way we want, by making a consistent but not excessive effort to direct them, and by rewarding and encouraging ourselves when they respond.

Emotional flashbacks are not necessarily as visually vivid as what we think of when we picture a war veteran returning from a combat-zone. You don't have to be diving for cover, waking up screaming, bursting into a rage, or suddenly crying your eyes out to be having an emotional flashback (we make no fun of those who find themselves doing these things: they are your fellow victims of trauma. We are just explaining a difference). Some abuse victims live in a semi-permanent state of thinking about, re-living and feeling again, what they felt during their time living with a narcissistic family member, spouse or partner. The activity of the brain in thinking these endless circles of thoughts is sometimes called 'ruminating', and it is a type of disassociating. Our thinking loops or repeats itself. It's usually negative and pessimistic, with an underlying sense of disaster or despair. Disassociation IS an emotional flashback!

When you are bothered, triggered or stressed by some situation, person or thing, and it makes you remember an event in an all-absorbing way that cuts you off from what's going on around you, your thoughts going around in a familiar order and your predominating response being an emotional flashback, then you're breaking off, disassociating yourself from the present, and turning inwardly to the past and your memories of trauma. You can't be there in the present moment if you are ruminating.

So, you find yourself ruminating, therefore you are having an emotional flashback. This is the time when you have to start becoming conscious of your need to carry out mental exercises to help you to deal with them. Look for what it was that set off your train of thoughts! It could be nothing more than tiredness... Your emotions are like letters sent from deep inside you, to your reasoning mind, telling you about something that's going on inside, even though the animal brain doesn't know exactly what it is. All people finding themselves ruminating often about their abuser would benefit from working on their flashbacks. Some people think they have, but they haven't!

You can be well-educated, even be a psychologist... and if you were traumatized by a narcissist (which can happen: nobody's automatically immune), you would need to identify, then confront and work through your trauma bond!

In the mind of every one of us, there is a sort of conversation or dialogue. From childhood, we have a sort of "parent's voice" reminding us of our obligations, expressing opinions about ourselves and other things. The famous psychologist Sigmund Freud would have called it the 'superego'. Then the world of our feelings and desires, sometimes half-visible, at other times hidden, often conflicted and confused, and very much living in our animal brain, which he termed the 'id'. Between all of this is a part of our personality which tries to decide what we are going to do, and how to balance the other two, which two, by their nature, are often in conflict. This, Freud called the 'ego'.

We need to become aware of this inner conversation, and silence some of the false and distorted things an abusive parent could have dinned into our youthful minds, at the same time as using reason to control the irrational instincts that tried to protect us, but have also been trapped and distorted. So, if you were to work regularly, daily, on identifying these voices, facing your feelings, and re-enforcing the truth about your life, your abuser and your future, you'd find yourself ruminating or remembering less vividly. If you achieve that after a couple of weeks, then you'll have proved to yourself that you were having flashbacks! No fear! You're actually dealing with them now!

Reader of this book: if you are a recovering victim of abuse, we have to warn you that your sessions with a therapist or counselor, or even your daily mindfulness, or writing in a diary, might cause you to have flashbacks! It's whatever your animal brain associates with the trauma, such as... thinking about it! This is the point: it's NOT a failure. We can tell people over and over and over again that they do need to confront certain thoughts and feelings in order to heal from them. If they pop up like mushrooms when you concentrate on a memory, then you are actually controlling them to a certain extent. You've pulled them out of the unconscious, into the cool light of day, when you are awake, and so able to use your rational brain...

So, not only are you seeing, but feeling your trauma-bond again. Now you can remind yourself:

- It wasn't my fault;

- Nothing my abuser said to insult me, is to be taken personally. Abusers just like to find hurtful things to say. THEY DON'T CARE IF IT'S TRUE OR NOT! Neither should I;

- I don't love the abuser. Love is mutual respect, and I never got that;

- I fell in love with the trauma bond! I fawned as a way to survive, just as I did when I was scared and hurt as a child, too little to be able do anything better;

- I cannot change an abuser by giving him or her what they want. Abusers, 'Narcs', just take, take, and take;

- I had to get away from my abuser. None of my staying on was doing me any good, and there is no way for me to help my abuser - other than to stay calm, get away, and cut off all contact. I truly desire to keep it like that;

- I have to be humble enough to get help when I need it. I am not alone: but I cannot do it alone;

- I may be tempted to go back to the relationship/family. If I am, I say: NO! I am a recovering addict. My 'narc-drug' will only make me sick again!

- Feeling down doesn't mean I'm going down!!

- I'm never going to regret taking my life back again!

Your rational brain is a wonderful thing, and one of the ways you'll use it to help you is to understand that THERE'S A DIFFERENCE BETWEEN WHAT I THINK, AND WHAT I FEEL. Some victims start to complain, and - not to be unpleasant - start to become critical and resistant to the other people in their support-group, their therapist, psychologist, or whoever they turned to for help. Often they are just saying, "But I don't feel anything good! I just feel it's the end of my life! I can't get myself to want to write in my diary!"

That's just our point. You have to! You do it because you understand that it's good for you, not because you feel like it! If you keep on, soon you will start to feel better. That will follow, though, after...

What other simple, straightforward things can you do? Remind yourself every day:

- Sleep enough! (Go to bed, not too early, but at the time you worked out is realistic. Even if you don't feel tired then. Then get up at the time you decided. Not necessarily before the rest of the world: that wouldn't make you better that the rest, nor is getting up later than 'average' making you worse. It's not a competition! Yet if you said 9 a.m., then 9 it must be.)

- Drugs and alcohol? They aren't medicines, and they aren't an escape. Don't use them; or in the case of alcohol, as we said, only with good company; and less than you are tempted to have!

- Eat good things - as in, healthy things - and drink enough water!

- Do your mental exercises and reminders!

- Get enough sunshine and exercise!

When you live like this, and you've washed, and dressed well, you will leave the house and realize that you've started to feel better. What won't help is to wait until you feel better, to start living well. Live well so that you can feel better later on!

People who have been broken down in any way by repeated traumatic situations lose their sense of having boundaries. As we saw, an abuser takes advantage of this. For example, she will get her husband to spend all day worrying about her concerns, while he neglects his. A victim of a trauma bond is someone who confuses his or her feelings of deep emotion for real love, again used by the abuser to get attention and power. When you have a better sense of yourself, you will be able to look at your feelings and understand them, rather than being driven back and forth. You will know how to agree to, or how to refuse a demand made on you by another person; and you will know how to agree to, or refuse, the feelings that rise up within you - and you will know the difference.

Chapter 15
There's a "Narc" in the Park! What a Narcissist Is, and Is Not

With all that has been said about trauma-bonding in this book, there's been a lot spoken about narcissists and narcissistic abuse. This is because these are often the people whose abuse usually leads to the formation of trauma bonds in the minds of their victims. That does not mean, however, that all abusers are narcissists. There are other types of personality who can traumatize, but attract, a vulnerable individual. The emphasis is on healing yourself, whatever the other person did, and whatever your experience was. However, it will help you to come to terms with and to get over what happened to you, to know a little bit more about what a narcissist is, and some other psychological conditions that can make life difficult for someone in any kind of relationship with them.

Narcissists are not, unfortunately, rare - but neither are they so common that we should go around in a sort of paranoid fear of them. It can happen that someone who is befriended by, then mistreated and tormented by, a narcissistic bully at school, becomes anxious and withdrawn when anyone tries to be friendly to him or to her as an adult. The emotional, animal brain is trying to protect that person from the possibility of this friendly approach being the 'love-bombing' of a sociopath in disguise. Such a victim needs to learn to trust again, to learn when that trust is appropriate, and what the signs of a narcissist might be. Likewise, someone who was in a trauma bond as an adult with Abuser A, doesn't want to fall for Abuser B in the future. To be healed within strengthens against the possibility of falling for someone too quickly and unthinkingly; and to know and understand what an abuser is like will help anyone to see the signs of a 'Narc' - a narcissist - much sooner.

Nobody is perfect. All of us have flaws, from little imperfections to deep faults. We are all sinners, to put it another way. Part of getting to know and trust someone, part of forming a relationship, is allowing them to see us as we are - with the danger of their seeing and disliking our "dark side". When we can do that, and the other person also responds by letting us see all of their flaws, we can be at peace with each other. Accepting the existence of another person's weaknesses and flaws is not to be blind to them, nor is it thinking that we could just tear into their life and cut out the bad parts. It is to love someone without condition. Love helps to see and set the boundaries of a relationship, helps two people to know what that relationship means.

Loving someone implies respecting them, and that isn't done by trying to force them into a mould called, "My Ideal Husband/Wife/Friend" or what you will. It is actually better to discover that the truth of who someone is, inside, is that he or she has some unpleasant parts; than to believe a beautiful lie about them... spun by that very person. The truth can heal you, but lies tie you into a bond - that is the case with a trauma bond!

Recovering from abuse happens when you, the victim, can be totally honest with yourself about what happened and accept that it happened. The truth will set you free.

Many narcissists started life as unhappy, abused children, though that's not always the case. Yet all of them came to a decision based on cynicism and despair, the conclusion that: "This is an evil world. I'll just take what I can get out of it, and if the truth doesn't get it for me, then I'll tell any lie that can do the job." They see significant others, who believe that means justify ends, that power is all you need, and decide to copy them. Power is wielded by binding others, and you bind people with lies... A narcissist is born. Some time between early childhood and mid-teens, it seems.

There is a common type of 'Narc' who, believing and choosing that truth doesn't matter, lives in a fantasy-world. Oops! Lots of us have a fantasy-world; but the difference here is that there are no personal boundaries and no respect of others (those are caused by love...). So, the whole wide world becomes a stage for Hero-Inn to stage his life-play. The people in his life, especially his closest victims, are the cast to co-star with him. It doesn't matter if the play is an action-thriller, a love-story, a tragedy, or even a comedy... it depends on who the 'Narc' is, and what stage of life he or she is in. Think of it: the action-thriller where Narc gets his excitement as he plays with his characters; the romance where he self-pleasures with the feelings of being loved and loving; the tragedy where he can cry his eyes out with self-pity at the things his worthless co-stars do to steal his happiness; or the sick comedy where he can laugh at the fact that they're all more pathetic than he is!

You are the actress, the actor, or just the stage-prop. You were chosen, dear victim, because you fit Hero-Inn or Hero-Inna's part. Probably your vulnerability made you easy to direct; your virtues made you a believable character, and the fact that you don't know what's going on, don't understand you're in a fantasy, means that you won't insult him or her by trying to re-write any of the lines! Your attempts to please Pre-Mad-Donna are your lines and your part. She insults you for not knowing what she wants, and your fumbling guesses are the funny lines she wants to hear. Then, she can despise you for being stupid when you get it wrong, feeling her goddess-like superiority, and later, take what you do when it's correct, as the service she deserves.

All narcissists are consumed with attention to themselves, so whether it's a fantasy-world they inhabit, or their place in the real world, the effect is alike. They use people. When their 'actors', and sources of money or sex or influence, or whatever, are no longer useful, or they've been damaged by the abuse, they throw them away.

So when it was said to you that you were in love with the trauma bond; that the 'love-bombing' phases of your roller-coaster relationship were fantasy, not truth; that the abuse was ugly and so was your abuser (no matter what his, or her physical beauty might be...), it was a way of showing you that you were a star in someone else's beautiful lie for themselves, and a sick tragedy for you! As you 'un-learn' your part in that play, the truth will set you free.

On the subject of stories: some narcissists tell tragic stories about themselves, as mentioned before, to find out who listens to them. They want people who can sympathize, and this is so that YOU can feel THEIR pain, so that YOU devote yourself to helping THEM. That's how their minds work. Some of these stories are lies, but not necessarily. It is a sad truth that some victims of war or family abuse turn into abusers themselves. They just find that their story gets them what they want. This is NOT to say that victims all turn into abusers, not at all! Unfortunately, there are some who choose lies over truth and power over love, and because they understand what it is like to be abused, they know how to abuse others. Knowledge is power; here, in a bad way.

There is an element of DISGUISE in narcissism (to continue the analogy of a play) which almost always has to be there at the beginning. You can hardly tell someone, "Hello. I'm a selfish bastard who would like to use you for my own benefit, and keep you for only as long as you are useful to me", and expect them to accept the offer, can you? Some narcissists, aging and collapsing within their personalities as, perhaps, they succumb to drugs and alcohol abuse, are more obvious, more pathetic. They can still wreak damage on people who are close to them. Especially a victim who has a trauma-bond with them! Yet their lies and wretchedness would make them easier to see for a potential victim, and so they are less dangerous to people who have just met them. Perhaps a tragedy is the only choice left to them to put on a 'costume' for, to play with people, to beg for sympathy and love because they have been "so badly treated" (their victims forgotten).

Narcissists can be male or female. However... their ready use of language and their complex social interactions, their sensitivity to fine differences in others' emotions and their common normal instinct to nurture very young children, make women generally good at being empathetic. Men know this, and so do women. However, the corruption of the best is the worst - and female narcissistic sociopaths can be dangerously manipulative. You cannot use someone unless you know them: and the ability to make other people open up, to see their side of things in a social interaction, can enable a woman of ill-will to control or influence others with ease. And to hide it! This is especially true in one-to-one and family relationships, where the focus, the 'stage' of the narcissist's play, is smaller but more detailed.

The use of children by a female sociopath is one of the most foul and horrifying types of narcissistic abuse. Unable to question or understand what is happening to them, children can become severely damaged as they are used as tools to gain control over a father, for instance. Some narcissists are so insecure and so jealous that they threaten to harm children if they don't get their way. We will never say that male narcissists cannot use children. We note, however, how deeply nurturing can be twisted subtly in the case of the primary caregiver of infancy, when a mother tries to teach her child to hate other caregivers: the father, the mother-in-law, for example. If she succeeds, it will increase her control of the child, and decrease their influence.

In adults, such control can be 'passive-aggressive'. For example, a 'Narc' can criticize her boyfriend by endlessly querying what he does, using the opinions of others. If he fixes the window with putty, she will say, "But my uncle uses silicone." Or she will ask him how to get rid of termites in the wooden shed. He will answer, giving the best way that he knows. Then, having heard his advice, she will say, "I think I'm going to ask at the hardware store." If he grows angry with her, and asks her how she knows what the best way is, if all she does is collect opinions, she will react with, "But I'm only trying to help you." Here is a problem: it is quite possible for someone to try to help in a rather passive way, by just giving advice that she - or he - has heard, only to burden the listener with what might be contradictory opinions. That could be from a genuine, if mistakenly acted-out, wish to help. What would make this NARCISSISTIC is the ill-will, the criticism, the expressed contempt, the intent to cause confusion and doubt, that this tactic might display, above all when done over long periods of time. A challenge to such a person, a confrontation with the fact that in these examples she doesn't actually know enough to criticize, might delay the boyfriend's slide into a passive, obedient state. However, being point-scorers in their games and playwrights in their plays, 'Narcs' are prompted to retaliate. She could play the 'yellow card' in this case, and accuse her boyfriend of having prejudice against women's knowledge, thereby demanding an apology, and sympathy; or she could attack him by accusing him of not having any technical qualifications to show on paper (a fact in this case, but not a proof of his having no knowledge). Notice the counter-accusation! In our example, the girlfriend will keep up this tactic often, and repeatedly, trying to make her boyfriend give up having confidence in his own work.

The words, "ill-will", "despise", "use", "hate", and so on, come up again and again with a narcissist. They simply do not love. You might put it that they love themselves, but if true love is reciprocal, then they haven't a clue. Many people have serious flaws in their characters. They may be violent, or depressed and crushed, or passive and complaining. Someone with similar inner wounds, especially from childhood, can be drawn to them and desire to heal their "inner child" together with their own inner child. Abuse can and does happen sometimes in these cases, but such abusers can and do have redeeming qualities. They may hate some people passionately, but they can and do love others. Narcissists are not like this. They are, can be demonstrated to be, simply cold and dead inside. They almost feed on the life and goodness of their victims. Victims often look back and feel that their abuser was somehow 'not there' inside, or that there was an overwhelming feeling of coldness and lack of affection most of the time in the relationship. There might have been sex, a lot of it at times, but no human warmth or connectedness.

If you are looking at this information from the outside, trying to help someone else who you know is a victim, and are trying to understand what kind of abuse has been happening, this characteristic of coldness and deadness is important. You probably won't know what it is like in the bedroom for your loved one, we are not silly enough to suggest that you ask. What you would see is this cold, contemptuous attitude. You can ask what the abuser is like when no-one else is there; whether, outside of their rewarding moods, there is any real warmth. In public, or in your presence, you should be able to pick up confusion tactics, or "mind-games" played by a 'Narc'. You might find that you are being treated as another actor, or a prop! Without drama (ironically), you need to resist playing in these games.

'Love' is truly a word narcissists don't understand. Often they will rush the beginning of a relationship, and use sex and excitement to create a bond. One feature that has been seen in narcissists is that they assume intimacy and friendship too quickly with anyone they want to impress: "Hey, buddy!" he says after you've met him and spoken to him for ten minutes! It's a trespassing of boundaries, it's pushing into your friend-ship-zone before time. Watch out! However, victims who bond with an abusive narcissist always see, sooner or later, that they were never as important to their abuser as their abuser was to them. The bond was with half of the 'Narc' and the whole of the prey! Narcissists are people for whom a promise or mutual agreement has little meaning in itself: it is thought of as a tool to get someone else to be bound to some act or understanding, but they act as if it had no obligation for them. Indeed, they can sometimes be openly contemptuous of "sticking to your word". Perhaps if a man lives with his girlfriend but has not married her, when he is exposed and confronted by his girlfriend's brother, proved to have had an affair with another woman... he merely replies coldly, "But I'm not married, am I?" The fact of there not being a public bond is used just as readily to excuse his behavior, as the fact of being married would be, if he were trying to get control of her property. This isn't a drifter or a 'commitment-phobe', it's a self-centered narcissist!

At this point, let us shine a light on recovery from a trauma bond with a sociopath who is a 'Narc'. (We just have to use that abbreviation, it's so handy!). It has to be thorough and it will be painful, like rebuilding your ability to have a relationship. That is just what you need to be able to have a capacity to love in peace, for the future. However, that process can change YOU for the better. There is a saying of Julian of Norwich that applies to you: "Though the soul's wounds heal, the scars remain. God sees them not as blemishes, but as honors." Think on that for a while...

To have no scars is to be AS IF IT HAD NEVER HAPPENED. When we are hurt, we may wish it could be healed like that. However, what is known about the way narcissists look for their victims, and the type of people who become such, shows us that you were wounded before you became entangled in the Narcissist's 'web'. You were injured in your earlier years. When you understand what happened to you and begin to take responsibility for your life, begin to understand what love is, then your experiences will help you to see what love is NOT, and your memories will become lessons instead of pains you cannot confront. You will be better than you ever were! A scar is a testimony of healing: it says literally, "There was a wound here." A scar is a promise to others that recovery is possible! In this way, without justifying abuse in any way, or denying its being evil, one of the most painful of human experiences can serve as an opportunity for you to become a better person than you were before you were abused, even though you were not responsible for the abuse.

There are some other convenient ways that may help you to identify a 'Narc', though there is no "one-size-fits-all" description. Human beings are complex, varied, individual, yet we have common traits and types of characteristics, shared by many but not by all; and other traits we all have because we are... human. You may feel like throwing up your hands in despair! Don't: you should be able to see a pattern, groups of different signs, in what has been mentioned in this book.

Here is the first of two small, important signs. For example, we mention the imagined case of Monnimyner, the narcissist who is busy 'conning' his employers, so that he's stealing thousands of dollars from them (we had better say, US dollars, to be clear about the severity). Yet one of Monnimyner's colleagues notices that boxes of instant coffee sachets are disappearing from the office canteen. Each box contains thirty sachets. One day she catches him putting a box into a plastic bag before he leaves work. He just says, "So what? Think of all the bonuses they make excuses not to pay us." There have been rumors about lost money coming from the accounts department, on the wider front. Soon after, Monnimyner is exposed and fired, and taken to court to try to recover the funds. It is relevant to mention that he will appear totally calm and unworried when he appears in court, in a way that no normal person, if guilty, would do. A normal person who is accused falsely, on the other hand, would also appear visibly upset, though one might be able to see that it is from shock, without shiftiness or evasion. Unfortunately, Monnimyner's cool, calm appearance and quickness to blame other people with careful working of the facts, will probably mean that his punishment will be lighter than that of another type of criminal with a normal state of mind. Or... just possibly, Monnimyner will do the opposite: he will break down, cry, and deliver a tear-jerking performance; admitting his guilt under desperate circumstances, so acted that it seems it was flavored with honey mixed with saccharine! Alas! Will the jury be duped? Why is it that normal people, be they innocent or guilty, do neither of these? Deep down is the reason: Monnimyner doesn't give a fig about what he's done. He feels nothing.

Now, continuing with the second part this story, because it has two parts: why was Monnimyner bothering to steal COFFEE SACHETS, maybe a few dollars' worth, when he hoped to get away with thousands of dollars in secret? This is what his former colleague is pondering. The reason seems to be exactly the same as the reason for the larger theft: BECAUSE HE COULD! Although a narcissist usually has the intelligence to realize that a small trespass might give him a bad reputation, when he is busy seeking to hide a much more important crime, his total dead calm makes people forget or doubt what they might come upon him doing. 'Narcs' know how to sow the seeds of doubt.
Yet we return to the mystery of this criminal type: they can well understand the difference between a small theft and a large robbery, but they cannot FEEL it. So sometimes they just 'do' a small theft. For the sake of it... and this COMBINATION is a sign of a narcissist.

An infamous example of a narcissist who betrayed someone whom he was supposed to love, and be under the authority of, is Judas Iscariot. Many people remember the story in the Bible of his betraying Jesus Christ for thirty pieces of silver. Enough to buy a small field; maybe, today, a tiny flat? Betraying someone does not necessarily make the betrayer a 'Narc': you could do it out of coercion, fear, desperation, anger: all bad reasons, but understandable. However, note that it was Judas who offered to do it, and asked them to make him an offer! He doesn't seem to have 'haggled' what he was offered any higher, did he? Note that he identified his victim with a kiss. A sign of affection! An act in his play, we realize. It can be seen that even as he was feigning friendship, Judas felt nothing.

104

This story also has its warning sign, its second part not so widely-mentioned or understood. The Gospel of John mentions the woman, desperate for forgiveness, who anointed Jesus with a jar of extremely expensive perfumed unction. Whereas the Gospel of Matthew mentions that "the disciples" and other people were shocked at the apparent waste of money, and complained, it's the Gospel of John alone that mentions how Judas was the main actor in this complaint. We are told that he declared that the money could have gone to the poor instead. And John adds the key observation: that Judas didn't care about the poor at all, but was a thief. He had charge of their common funds, and would steal out of the purse. The 'Narc' revealed! Why steal, when following and working with someone who was known for being able to see through you and into you, into your heart? Because Judas could! Might he have added, "Well, He didn't stop me, did He?"

Understand that this observation was made by the youngest of the team of disciples, just a youth at the time. Often it is, as we mentioned before, a small-part actor in a narcissist's life-fantasy play who stumbles on telling and important evidence. So if you are on the outside, looking at a relationship that looks to be toxic, and want to judge the apparent abuser, look for small signs as well as serious cruelty or bad attitudes, and small observations by bystanders who are observant.

Another way to get knowledge of someone's 'Narc' personality is, some psychologists point out to us, simply to refuse one of their requests - politely and without anger. Don't snap, don't sigh, don't look gloomy, don't look afraid. It needs to be a request for something fairly small, something that most people ask every day. Maybe, "Pass me the butter, please?" (whether or not 'Narcs' use the word 'please'). Even try smiling! What happens?
"What *** **** are you saying? No?"
"Are you crazy?"
"Why? What's wrong with you?"
"Whaddayou mean by, 'No'?" "Didn't you hear me?"

If you get these reactions, if the other person flies into a rage, you have unmasked a narcissist! This is because they do not recognize the boundaries between themselves and others, at least not in the sense of rights or self-direction. Other people are there to serve them, they think. Their wishes are to be other people's wishes. It is as if the famous genie, who appears and says, "Your wish is my command", has had his words twisted - and the 'Narc' glides up and says, smiling, "My wish... is your command."

When you refused the wish of the narcissistic personality, you put up a boundary, asserting that you can accept or reject that person's commands. In other words, that you have a will, a separate will from the will of the 'Narc'. That's like a declaration of independence; in his or her eyes, like a declaration of war!

Underneath so much of their exploitativeness, envy, self-pity and bitterness, narcissistic personalities have a sense of entitlement. You should be able to judge this from the words and opinions of your abuser, if you've been in a relationship with one. They never seem to have an obligation to pay taxes or subscriptions; the seethe with anger when other people (even, other 'Narcs') have privileges or money. They sneer at the privileged for thinking that they might be better than the rest of us; and then demonstrate that they think they're better than anyone else! When they attain success in worldly terms, they promptly justify exploitative, harsh or dishonest practices with the refrain, "But it's in our interests." At the bottom of these attitudes is a basic belief that the world owes them a living, in other words, that they're entitled.

There are other entitlement-obsessed people in the world whom we might not class as narcissistic sociopaths. Some are lazy, complaining, bitter, or self-righteously angry. They sponge off relatives, and resent being told they'll have to find work, otherwise they will not qualify for social security payments. Narcissists may do all these things, but these complainers don't steal coffee-sachets; they can love other people who love them; and they can give them gifts without doing it as a way to get something out of their loved ones! Yes, they have problems, but they aren't cold, dead 'Narcs'. Someone who is a 'rescuer' could end up in a trauma bond with a 'sponger', one may suppose, hoping that he or she will come to life and stop being bitter. There may or may not be a future for such a relationship, we cannot judge here; of course, what we are saying to everyone who is trauma-bonded, is that they need to heal themselves.

Gifts were just mentioned. Narcissists will take and use gifts given to those around them without hesitation. Often just mean to others, one can understand that actually, they do sometimes give gifts to other people. The problem for those people is that the gift always seems to have "strings attached". They use the giving as a means to confuse the victim they insulted yesterday; they might give in public, to validate their public image. Or else the "strings" are feelings of obligation the recipient is meant to have towards the abuser. For example, he demands that she go with him to live in Canada. She protests that they don't know anyone there. He rants, "I just gave you that diamond necklace you always wanted, and now you treat me like this!"

We hope that these considerations will be of help to you, the victim. Unfortunately, it isn't possible to "diagnose" a narcissist as a doctor would diagnose kidney-stones. Counseling sessions with that abusive partner, assuming that an abuser can be convinced to attend them, can be turned into "Hello, Ms. Shrink; I'm SO glad to meet you", charm-offensives. It is necessary to have a good amount of humility when dealing with such a person professionally, because they can and do deceive professionals. After all, if the other client is an abuser after all, then he or she is a lying, manipulative bastard who is trying to deceive their partner. So will the abuser not try to hide those attitudes?

The last topic to be covered in this chapter on discerning whether or not you are dealing with a narcissistic sociopath, is to explore the fact that some people who have ASPERGER'S Syndrome are misunderstood and thought to be narcissistic types, and that most of the time this is totally, tragically mistaken.

The behavior that is called "Asperger's Syndrome" seems to be a mild to moderate case of autism. Severely-affected autistic people may be almost unable to communicate, may live as if in a world of their own, rocking backwards and forwards. We are definitely not dealing with such a degree of retardation. It is enough to consult the many articles that have been written on this subject to see that there is a cluster of certain types of behavior, which, if someone displays, makes it to be likely that one is dealing with this problem.

Does this person like to repeat certain acts or insist on certain routines, almost obsessively? Do they often seem to be daydreaming, talking to themselves, imagining vividly, maybe even rocking before going to sleep? Do they hate sudden loud noises, wearing bright-colored clothes or tight clothing? Do they seem to be very unemotional - or suddenly burst out with violent but fearful reaction? Are they awkward in social situations, shy, but also capable of one-liners or sudden outbursts? Can they be tactless and direct, basically truthful but unable to judge appropriate contexts? Do they misunderstand expressions, e.g. to "kick the bucket", taking it literally? Do they rarely look at you when you talk to them, and almost never when they talk to you? Are they interested in a particular subject or subjects which form an obsession, so that they become extremely knowledgeable, perhaps, and on which the most verbal of them can talk rapidly and forcefully - yet forget and confuse themselves in other subjects? Are they deeply affected by sound: very musical, perhaps, or obsessed with like of, or dislike of, certain noises?

Other features might be: extremely slim build (or possibly its opposite, very robust); lack of physical co-ordination; or else excellent co-ordination but with terrible over-correction; digestive and nasal problems; skin problems including over-sensitivity to touch and feel, or insensitivity to physical damage; a fearful nature regarding physical danger, or its opposite - a reckless taking of risks without seeming to understand the likelihood of an accident? Have they irregular growth of hair and unusual fingerprint patterns? Does this syndrome sometimes run in families?

Well, this is a list of all sorts of things people have observed, though there is disagreement regarding some. Note the infuriating tendency for some to be opposites, e.g. to be almost unable to talk, or almost unable to shut up! Some balance seems to be thrown out, either one way, or the other, in their constitution. Scientists don't know yet what the exact cause is.

This book is about trauma-bonding, so we cannot go too far. It is enough to say that the greatest problem with regard to people with Asperger's, and trauma-bonding, seems to be that they attract people who have been traumatized as children; or that, because they seem odd and can be irritating and confusing, THEY are traumatized in childhood. Yet, difficult as that may be for both sides, it is not just that; another question lurks in the background: IS THIS PERSON A NARCISSIST?

Why would you think so? Well, 'Narcs' hide a lot of themselves. So do these people. They can seem to be cold, rational and unaffectionate - or else go into 'meltdown' and fly into a rage. They can seem uninterested and switched off when you share something with them. On another occasion, infuriatingly, they can suddenly recall the slightest detail of what happened, even though they seemed not to be paying attention at the time! Those who have more social skills may seem rude, arrogant, over-sensitive and proud. Why? It can be seen why - they have been hurt, often, and some may try to protect themselves behind this shell. Oh, and can we forget... at unexpected moments, unpredictably, they suddenly show great affection and emotion in some cases, maybe cry for half an hour (grown men with a tendency to stay silent in large groups!), or talk scintillatingly and to amuse in conversation, and be very kind! "He's 'love-bombing me, isn't he?" you hear a frightened voice screaming in your head.

It is much more likely to be a male than a female, though female sufferers do exist.

So...? The answer is, if you go back to the behavior and signs listed above, which are characteristics of Asperger's Syndrome, then it is unlikely. If he has Asperger's traits, be kind to him and think of Asperger's! Some sufferers are so unaware of social conventions, so unable to understand lying, and must work so hard to concentrate, that they are just not going to be capable of manipulative, covert narcissism.

We are dealing with two very different conditions; one voluntary (a decision to use hate and seek power), the other manifesting involuntarily in early childhood, and causing much pain and confusion to the sufferer. They can both confuse you, but what touches on 'Narcs' is their endless contempt, and ill-will to all beings other than themselves. Asperger's sufferers can both hate and love people; sometimes they can be found loving a pet or other animal, with deep awareness. They may misunderstand many people, but understand some; and when things are explained to them logically, how they should or should not behave, usually they will accept it surprisingly calmly. A 'Narc' would start shouting threats or crying for pity!

We cannot, in a subject as complex as human affairs, say categorically that no Asperger's sufferer, above all a mild case, has ever been a malignant narcissist. Just possibly, with his tendency to obsess, his private world (very much an escape from this sad world that he is so aware of...) and some extremely good skills that make up for his handicaps in other ways, he might become a sociopath with dangerous capabilities. But even in that case, then, ask yourself simply, "Is this a narcissist?" If he has 'Narc' traits, be realistic about him and think of narcissism!

One of the main communication-problems with Asperger's sufferers who are in relationships is that they may seem to have no empathy. Some may even say that they don't want love-relationships. What can be seen is that an Asperger's sufferer is a human being who can have and understand feelings but struggles to know what other's, even his own, are. He, or she, may need explanation rather than silent treatment or hints. Those are tactics doomed to fail on these people! (By the way, not to hurt you, but those are rather 'Narc' tactics!). Do they not like touch? Well, if by that you mean the friend who comes up behind you and pokes you in the ribs, then no - you might end up being punched in the stomach. Almost like a wild animal, their instincts of danger are often quick (or horribly lacking in others!) and their feeling of pain or fear is more intense than average. On the other hand, they may respond to a massage from a partner with ecstasy, and be very good at giving one. It is the uncontrolled touch they don't like. They may hate noises at night, and then listen to 'heavy metal' music at high volume on the sofa.

Again, they are in a place they know, with controlled, intense, known sounds.

Lastly, women who love men with this personality may complain: he's not romantic; he hates surprise parties, he hates giving or accepting gifts. The last two, yes. They do not like sudden change. They may lose control; or just bear with it and handle it, as a necessary evil. Your surprise party... They find giving hard if it isn't a logical need. Why not have some money to get what YOU want? As for romantic: if you mean, anticipated, sensitive, creative, stand-in-your-shoes surprises, attention that is playful but not too intense... perhaps you had better accept that this is unlikely. Do you love him, or her? You'll have to accept... just as you must accept yourself to heal yourself. Can you change him? You can help him, teach him something, understand him, but NO, you cannot 'magic' Asperger's away. Why not be thankful for what he is, and does? Or he may just be too hard for you, in your present state of exhaustion and need for healing, to handle. If so, that you will need to accept.

WHEN NARCISSISTS CAVE IN ON THEMSELVES

When trying to understand and identify people with narcissistic tendencies, not only are there different types of them (Covert Narcissists, Grandiose Narcissists, and so on), different degrees of their ill-will ("malignant narcissist" describes a dangerous and highly damaging individual), but there are also different stages in their lives.

Obviously, using people to gratify your desires and needs isn't healthy for the victims, whatever type the abuser is! The fact is, of course, that living like this takes its toll on the narcissist as well. People in general start to find out what they are really like; victims either become so damaged that they aren't useful any more (or maybe the money runs out...) and new victims have to be found. Actually, as noted before, the 'Narc' is addicted to victimizing, so that engaging in negative, destructive, critical behavior becomes a way of life. A scam or a trick in business can be repeated if you keep moving from one city to another; eventually you might run out of new places you are familiar enough with, or the excitement of making money "for nothing" wears thin, leaving the 'Narc' with the choice of trying something bolder and yet more dangerous, or else trying something totally new.

We also mentioned that a significant number of "Cluster B" personalities, people with narcissistic or anti-social tendencies, become addicts not just of abusing others emotionally, but also of alcohol, drugs, or engaging in risky, unhealthy or promiscuous sex. These habits also enslave and take their toll on the abuser's mental and physical health. Lastly, there is growing old: it happens to us all, but to face it without good looks or the charm of youth (when you used these to lie your way through life), and with the addictions and bad habits mentioned affecting your vitality, makes aging a heavier burden for such people.

When they are older and failing in their ability to use other people (their "narcissistic supply" as it is known, is decreasing), then narcissists may experience a physical or mental breakdown. Alternatively, they just become bitter, angry and miserable. Psychologists call such a person a "Collapsed Narcissist". To identify someone in this state may be easier if you have been in the unfortunate situation of knowing them over time. If you've just met or started interacting with them only recently, they may be harder to identify. If so, take care! They've not necessarily committed the most serious physically abusive behavior, or turned to drink, though we mentioned that they do so quite often. A less "destroyed" but simply aging 'Narc' may look more friendly or unthreatening.

Nothing said before implies, dear victim or interested reader, that such a person is harmless. They may be weakened, but they are also desperate; their failing enjoyment of life makes them deeply resentful, turns them into killjoys with a desire for vengeance, and yet drives them to try to make other people feel pity for them.

A closer look at "collapsed narcissists" is done best with an illustration of some traits which are typical of women, and then those typical of men. We believe that a greater number of them will be women, for no other reasons than because: women live somewhat longer than men, tend to abuse alcohol and drugs less often, or in lesser amounts; and are better at hiding their narcissistic behavior during life, so that it becomes obvious only in old age. Male collapsed 'Narcs' exist, and are disgusting and dangerous, too, it goes without saying. In Chapter 23: QUESTIONS, ANSWERS AND CASE-STUDIES, you can read two fictitious case-studies to show what these types of narcissistic characters can be like. Keeping in mind the basic theme of this book: would anyone be in a trauma bond with such a person? The fact is, that it is possible. A faithful, crushed spouse of many years, a passive, depressed child, or a traumatized grandchild in difficult circumstances, could end up trying to love such an individual through the years despite getting nothing good in return.

At the end of this examination of what features identify narcissists, we can say again that individual cases of 'narc'-type behavior vary a lot, but there are remarkable similarities wherever you go throughout the world. The last chapter of this book, already mentioned, includes more true-to-life stories to illustrate some of the different varieties of sociopathic abuse by narcissists, all of which would be serious abuse.

If you have trauma-bonded with a narcissist, now you know the monster. They're evil. If you trauma- bonded with a fellow-victim, be they abused, Asperger's... or just a selfish character with some redeeming qualities... whatever you decide to do, now you know you're not dealing with a monster, but with a lesser problem! You still have a problem, though. Yet the way to fix any of these problems is, first and foremost, to carry on with your mission to grow and be healed in yourself.

Chapter 16
Healing After Sexual Abuse and Domestic Violence

S o many times in this book, the word 'abuse' has been used. You will have understood that it referred to shouting, criticizing, being ignored, lying and mental tactics, and so much more; and physical injury has been mentioned, but not in detail.

Dear reader, are you here at this point, tense and yet relieved, because at last someone has mentioned sexual abuse? Or, was your physical abuse far more severe than a slap on the face? Have you been permanently scarred, or were you afraid for your life?

We have written all of the chapters to help victims of abuse, whatever form it took. At this point, let us consider those who have experienced any form of sexual contact, inappropriate behavior, talking or viewing, in childhood...

Yes, you were abused. You don't need to qualify it by saying that "it wasn't penetrative" if it was still sexual. Nor do you need to tone down the seriousness of what was done to you if your abuser stopped of his or her own will, perhaps when you were old enough to realize what was going on; nor can you forget it, if your abuse stopped because you told a family member, and your abuser was not allowed to be alone with you thereafter... but the subject was never spoken of again.

Things that you learn on your way to being an adult, and not all in one day either, are not meant for small children. So, you feel guilty, don't you? So many victims grow up with a sense of guilt or shame; and this is a very particular, very body-related shame.

IT WASN'T YOUR FAULT. No child understands what it all means, even when he or she is old enough to have some idea of what sexual intercourse is. You see, the trouble with our brains - as has been

114

mentioned many times in this book - is that they try to protect us, but do so in the animal part of the brain, and it is irrational.

When, as a child, you broke a window because you were careless about where you played with a ball, your parents shouted at you, no doubt, and gave some form of punishment. This is quite normal and reasonable. Windows aren't made to be broken, and when they are, the pieces of glass are dangerous. As a result of seeing and hearing the broken window, and the punishment you got afterwards, you would have felt a sense of guilt. So, afterwards, when you played with the ball again, the feeling of shame would have made you more careful, and you would have made sure that you played in another place. This is called 'conditioning' and it's a part of learning about the world. Your rational brain was informed about this rule of not playing near windows, but far more, the learning of that bad feeling took place in the animal brain.

What happens if, for example, one of your parents begins to touch you and undress you in a strange way? Not only that, but threatens to get you into trouble if you tell anyone? To your animal brain, you start to feel the same kind of shame and avoidance. Yet you can't really avoid your parents... Your rational brain knows that you are punished by your parents at times, and also thinks that this must be another such situation. The result: SHAME.

How much more if you were violated, injured, saw a side of your parent - or any significant other - that was their animal side? Saw or felt what people will normally only experience much later, and on their own, in their own bodies, at puberty? You will be horribly confused. If such behavior was made worse by threats, you would have experienced "cognitive dissonance" - as mentioned, the contradiction that the people or person who gives you the roof over your head, your food and drink, and teaches you about things - also treats you so that you feel pain, confusion and shame.

As you grow older, and realize what happened to you, your shame will only grow. Most victims decide to try to forget it all, try never to think about it or speak about it. You probably did. Occasionally, victims do speak to someone, but that person's reaction of horror and shame, and perhaps the experience of being begged never to mention it again, puts them off talking about it.

Victim - you need to speak to someone who will listen. These worst kind of traumas in childhood do not just go away. They can cause pain and confusion for years - and no doubt you know that is true. So many complexes, fears, addictions, and problems in relationships - not least, the danger of forming a trauma-bond with a narcissist when you are an adult - result from sexual abuse as a child.

We can say, to comfort you, that all of the advice given in this book, and the steps needed to understand what happened to you, to change the way you think and feel, and to recover from any trauma in your life, are not radically different in your case. Yes, you can overcome the shame and avoidance! It is never, never too late to start a healing process, even if you are old now.

Yet, you must speak to someone you can trust. It may be hard to do so, but if you do, you will have begun the journey of healing. Men, above all, who were victims of childhood sexual abuse, need to realize that they need to talk about it to someone who is trustworthy. Don't fool yourself by saying that, "I can handle it. I'm an adult now." No! When you were abused, you were a minor, a child unable to process the thoughts and feelings you were subjected to. We tend not to deal with deep traumas. In that way, we don't grow in that area, because it never gets any attention. Deep in a part of you, you are still a little boy in shame and fear and confusion. You need to get that out into the light of adulthood, and admit it, think clearly what exactly it was that was done, understand it, and then use your reason, and some sympathetic help, to see that it is all in the past.

Some online, internet-based support groups might help you to start talking about what happened. They can be anonymous. You will need to come to a point where you can talk about it in person when you have the opportunity. Perhaps you need to explain what happened to you, to family members who knew nothing about your abuse. Firstly, though, if you are not sure of the reaction from some of them, then you need to speak to a good counselor or therapist first (don't forget the parent or adult relative, who wasn't your abuser as such, but who knew about it and kept quiet, perhaps also being controlled, threatened by, and bonded to your abuser... was also a kind of guilty party). You have every right to ask that expert about his or her personal method, beliefs or experience: you need to be able to trust them, to know what their 'world-view' is, and if you are comfortable with it.

Recovery is hard; but as it begins, recovering victims tell us that they soon start feeling improvement. Recovery takes time, but it is worth it, they agree; and not just by the end of the counseling process!

Bitterness and anger are natural responses to injury. You will experience these feelings at some point, if you haven't done so already for years... Yet the way to heal is, just as for other victims, to deal with the past, to accept it... and let go. You will learn how to make the most of the present, and of the future. You lost some of your past to your abuser: don't let him or her take away your present, let alone your future! When, after a bit of caring, guided introspection, you can put your focus once more onto the present (which is the place where you get things done!) and on the future, you will no longer be a victim, but a survivor.

DOMESTIC VIOLENCE

Physical violence to your person as a child is hardly less damaging than sexual abuse, and if that was your experience, you also need compassion and understanding. Growing up with such treatment, an atmosphere of fear and suspicion will usually result, and many victims of this type of abuse also feel shame and worthlessness, and that their bodies are objects, separate from them, or ugly. Problems in adulthood that can manifest if you feel this way about yourself can vary. Some victims do grow up to be violent themselves, to think that violence is the best - or the only - way to solve personal disagreements. However, if the violent parent or caregiver is narcissistic and manipulative, his or her efforts to crush the victim's independence and initiative usually make that person passive and depressed. Depression is, in a way, ANGER

117

TURNED INWARDS. This anger with themselves can make victims seek to numb their disappointment and pain with alcohol or drug abuse, overeating, sexual escapism or denying themselves food - anorexia. Others harm themselves. It can be observed that there is a sub-culture in fashion to wear dark, gloomy clothes, to use make-up to look pale and ill, or to have a great number of tattoos, body-piercings and distortions of ears, nose, and so on; to look aggressive and anti-social. We are not trying to judge any one individual here, but we can ask the question: Are these people not expressing fear, shame and discomfort with their own bodies?

It has been said before; we repeat: victims of abuse - sexual or domestic physical violence - tend to end up in abusive or violent relationships as adults. The feelings in such relationships are so well-known to victims since their youth, and a sense of unworthiness drives those who are abused as children to accept the unacceptable, telling themselves that they will have to tolerate it, of there being no other option. How wrong can you be!! Yet you know now and understand that in a trauma-bond, your brain is holding you captive, and that these irrational ties to your abuser can and should be broken.

Also said before, is that if your life or health is in danger, you need to make plans and get away to a place of safety. Once you've done that, you need to find legal protection. If you and your 'Narc' partner have children, that's going to be all the more necessary. A narcissist who loses his victim is going to be enraged. Saying this isn't fear-mongering, just being realistic. It was realistic to leave a violent husband or boyfriend who trapped you into a cycle of abuse and trying to get you to love him; you must just continue thinking realistically. Though at this point we are discussing a male narcissistic sociopath, we are aware of the narcissistic rage of a female abuser; and do not deny her malice, either, manifested in less physical but just as toxic ways. Especially if there are children involved.

'Narcs' are also addicts! This is an unpleasant fact of their human brains. Just as you, the victim, became dependent on your abuser and trauma-bonded with them, becoming attached and even feeling something like love or pity despite your abuse; so they, too, become ad-dicted to their "narcissistic supply". If these people are cold and dead on the inside, they live through their victims: getting attention, showing their supposed "superiority", forcing submission to them and adoration to be given them. Their addiction is like the case of the endlessly-argu-ing couple where one seems to be dominant. These do not necessarily involve a narcissist, but are unhealthy all the same. If 'Bossy Bessy' spends years criticizing her husband, confusing and ordering him about with noisy commands while he remains complaining and passive... the typical pattern, if he dies first, is that she becomes broken and de-pressed, and grieves deeply. Why? She became dependent on having him to validate her, prove her right, make people fear her, or feel sorry for her - and now he's gone!

...And now YOU'VE gone! 'Narcs' without their victims are like 'rehab' patients, except that they aren't in this position willingly. Their self-pit-ying rage can be dangerous, no less in the case of those whose health and intelligence are being eaten away by substance-abuse, than in the case of clever and ill-willed manipulators. Kicking, biting, trying to choke their victim, beating and any kind of mental threat are not be-neath a man who has done any of these things in the past. You need the support of a shelter for abused women, for example, a support-group, and any friends and family who are really sympathetic. Here we de-scribe legal protection, and the way you need to think and behave to make the best of it, and stay strong emotionally.

Victims of abuse may find dealing with legal professionals difficult. In the court, for example, the professionals have no reason to be afraid! They haven't lived with a monster - you did! Not only that, but a narcis-sist in trouble with society will try to be as charming as possible, as we saw before. You need to be strong and describe what happened to you as carefully as you can. Any evidence you have is important, but even if you don't have physical scars, just tell the truth as it was. You know in-side you that the truth is the truth - you were abused. Don't despair! Yes, you will tell your side, and he, his side. Remember that these peo-ple have a lot of experience in dealing with cases like yours.

If you succeed in getting a "restraining-order" or other legal instrument to protect you, there is a strong possibility that a narcissist will try to trespass on it. Such people see their ex-partner as 'property', and that they have a 'right' to see you whenever they want. They have little or no respect for the law; you will just have to steel yourself for the appearance in court. They will know it's stressful for you; what you have to do is to be calm and to convince the court not by emotions, but just the facts. You were abused... you don't need to do any "mental gymnastics" like your abuser. Just tell it the way it was!

In court or other situations where they are examined, narcissistic sociopaths will leave out little bits of a story, change small details, or say some things very quickly, hoping that the court will not notice. Good lawyers will stop them, ask them to repeat, or clarify apparent contradictions. If you have the chance to speak, make your side of these things clear. Narcissists are so grown used to twisting the truth: by accusing you of what they really did, of retaliating, that it is quite possible for a victim to get a restraining order, only for the abuser to try to get one from his or her side! A narcissist may break down in tears and claim that YOU are the abuser, especially in the case of a female 'Narc', using emotional drama to try to get sympathy. Men do it as well. It's called 'projecting'. Everything they do - forcing you to do all the work at home, hitting you with a broomstick, taking the money from your bank account if you have a separate one... will be thrown back at you. You, the 'Narc' will allege, never did any housework, hit him with a broomstick, and stole all the money out of his account and spent it! You have to be clear-headed, and to explain what is happening. Stick to the facts!

All of these difficulties are named, not to put you off - they serve to warn you, once again, to stay far, far away from a narcissist! In cases where that person is potentially very dangerous, it would help to be in a place far away and unknown to them. On the other hand, if you live in a community with better social networks and support, and you have a chance of being happier there, it will be harder to avoid a 'Narc' but you would have more support. This, you and the people who are your support-network, must decide.

In circumstances when there is a divorce or separation, and the couple concerned have children, it is normal to want them to spend time with both parents. Those are normal, not 'narc' circumstances. We understand that it is difficult for children to experience a break-up, and when in this book we repeatedly advise victims to leave abusers, it is not saying that relationships, in general, are nothing, or should be broken lightly. Rather, we are saying that toxic, bonded relationships with a narcissistic partner are not real bonds of love and family, and that if one parent is the victim, the children will be as well. If it is possible to prevent children from seeing an abusive, manipulative or unloving parent, please do so! We also believe that in the majority of these sociopathic cases, the children would want this as much as, or more than, their trauma-bonded parent!

If you read this chapter as the relative or loved one of a victim, you may very well be in a rage because of the things done to them. You may want to retaliate. It's only natural, but...

Given what we have said, how they retaliate, justify themselves, project, live off the stress and trauma they cause, and so forth, if you try to attack the abuser, it risks putting your loved one in more danger. You may be tempted to go too far. Put your focus on your significant other. Your role in this is to PROTECT and care for them. A victim who has someone like you is very blessed, because not all of them are so fortunate. You can be vigilant, and make sure that the abuser stays away. The idea that apparent indifference is the best strategy, applies to you. You won't help your loved one if you start a screaming match! That would be weakness of a sort: showing publicly that you are disturbed, out of control, upset. You, too, need to maintain a calm, cool approach and give away no unnecessary information.

This has been a chapter of hard facts and situations that someone recovering from a trauma bond may have to face. Look at it from this point of view: EVERY REALITY THAT YOU HAVE TO FACE AND DEAL WITH IS A WAY TO BREAK YOUR TRAUMA BOND with your abuser. After going through legal procedures, you will be stronger inside, and more able to see abuse for what it was. You are becoming a survivor!

Chapter 17
Control Your Emotions to Start Being Free

T his book has reached a point where it is time to start looking at what you are going to do to get out of a toxic situation, and once out (if you are not already), not try to carry it around inside you.

To prepare yourself, one of the important things to do is to control your responses to situations, and not just react to them in the heat of the moment. This is how...

For all of your life, your animal brain has been reacting rapidly - which it does by nature - to any kind of aggression or danger or insult. It's almost second nature; in fact, it's an instinct. So: what do you do when someone shouts at you? Shout back? That's likely. Or cringe and start shaking? That's also likely when one thinks of the way narcissists intend to crush and control the people around them. Soon the fear and trembling happens every time you are insulted, and it's part of your trauma-cycle. It's automatic, unconscious. Often we don't think about our reactions at all - we just... ...react.

Yet you have a rational, thinking brain as well; the largest part of the brain, indeed! How does the rational brain work? By RESPONDING, taking a little time to think. Response is something you do consciously, trying to be objective, and in the present. Because it is working in the here-and-now, conscious response has to do with making choices.

How often we merely react, and feel idiotic or upset by our words or deeds! You just have to think about what happens, for example, when you are driving and someone steps into the road too quickly. You have to slam on brakes and stop. Then, after shouting at them, once he or she has crossed over, you react by slamming your foot on the accelerator. You skid the tires and go charging off, only to realize there's a cross-roads with red traffic lights ahead, so a split second later you have to slam the brakes on again. By this time there is a crowd of people looking at you, and you've turned yourself into a spectacle. Embarrassing! There is a lot of shame in trauma, isn't there?

To train yourself to handle life better from now on, you need to respond, by learning how to "respond rather than react". It's not a one-off. Breaking out of a trauma-bond, let's face it, is a process. It's hard work - but work you won't regret.

So, give yourself space. You slammed on the brakes because you had to. What followed was NOT inevitably instinctive; you had a choice. As busy as some people think they have to be, take a second to STOP and think; just to be aware of what to do next. In this example, put your foot on the accelerator normally...

Train yourself to look at things objectively. This doesn't have to take a long time. Enough here to say to yourself: "It's over now." Therefore, there is no need to charge off. You did shout at the pedestrian, so this person knows that he or she acted dangerously. There is a subtle and dangerous tendency for us to read things into situations, especially motives; have you ever been in that pedestrian-and-motorist situation and caught yourself believing that the pedestrian walked into the road DELIBERATELY to force you to stop, and does your reason not tell you that this is really unlikely? It's a habit you've fallen into, how many of us do it... but we can and should practise being objective. Gradually we'll stop seeing the world through yellow-jaundiced glasses!

Take a moment to breathe deeply if you can. Your body reacts to sudden shocks with increased heartbeat, shallow, quicker breathing and the like. If you breathe deeply, willing yourself to slow down, your heart-rate will go down, your production of stress-hormones will drop, and you will be less likely to burst out in anger and say something you'll regret afterwards. Your thoughts will become clearer and more rational.

That is the method. Basically, you are going to re-train yourself to deal with unpleasant or angering or frightening situations by responding mindfully. You'll be as if standing on the sideline, your reason watching your thoughts and feelings, and taking over when things get out of hand.

So what about when you've just come screeching to a halt for the second time in thirty seconds? When you've reacted blindly again? Forgive yourself! Learning a new skill takes time. If you walked with a limp and a skewed leg all your life (which in a way you have...), when you have an operation to straighten your bent leg, afterwards you will need to re-learn to walk. To stand upright and make equal paces. So it is with becoming mindful of your emotions. You don't whip them into obedience; instead, you train them to obey your reason, with practice.

Chapter 18
Break the Bonds!

C ONGRATULATIONS! You've left the narcissist. That is the first step; they are predators, and you had to get out to start living. If the narcissist left you? CONGRATULATIONS! You may be feeling awful, but this is actually a blessing in disguise. Now, having explained previously in earlier chapters more about what abusers are, let us concentrate on breaking the bonds that are still holding you inside.

People are individuals, so your situation may look somewhat different to what was described in previous chapters, but the basic facts and the solution to your trauma are the same.

Firstly: break off all contact with your abuser! Yes, there may be difficulties, financial, legal regarding children... but this is the best way!! Not just, don't meet the narcissist: but don't text him, receive e-mails from him, follow his doings on social media, or talk about him with other people who are in contact with him. Don't keep his letters or e-mails (if you need them as evidence of abuse, can you not print them, seal them in an envelope and give them to a lawyer - or to a friend, to give you when the time comes to see a lawyer?) If he gave you gifts when he was love-bombing you, give them away, sell them... anything that triggers memories of that person.

In the case that you and the abuser have children, and there is a question of custody, do the following: be as unemotional as you can, and don't give any information. Don't even bother to give away that you are feeling better, when you are! They'll try to undermine it. Give them nothing...

Though the memories are in your mind, they are almost physical... in your body and your surroundings, and almost spiritual... in your very deepest level of being. So this is why a recovering victim needs to be really thorough to overcome them.

Next: using the TRUTH, overcome all the lying and confusion you've been attacked with. Repeat to yourself that you went through hell, that your abuser is messed-up, dangerous, and has an ugly personality. You don't need him or her, and they don't deserve your attention ever again!

Write down everything your abuser ever did to you, starting with the worst things. Have it in front of you and keep reading it, especially when you are reminded of the 'good' times you thought you had with them occasionally.

Some people recommend keeping a journal of your daily life at the present moment, to help you to see your progress. Vent your feelings in it! Maybe it will be easier to record your voice, than typing or writing.

Another, deeper way of coming to terms with what you went through is actually to write it as a story. Write it as if it's a book about someone else's life, but it will be yours. Ghostwrite your own life! Name the characters however you want. You will find yourself remembering all sorts of things, so put them down. All of this will help you to be kinder to yourself, and yet tougher and more objective regarding your circumstances.

You need to practise MINDFULNESS. Keep trying consciously to live in the present moment. Your brain, you know, is obsessed with pain, and you have a lot of pain in your past. So you have to stop it from pulling you back there, and keep it focused on the present, which is where you are working to fix things for yourself. Your brain also needs to focus on pleasure, so look after yourself and do things you enjoy.

Narcissists literally hypnotize people in a relationship, and their victims end up believing they are in a bubble, sometimes pleasant and sometimes awful, a sort of parallel universe. Fight that foggy feeling and stay objective. It's hard, but it's simpler than all that nonsense!

One of the most painful moments in breaking free is shortly after you leave the relationship, most people have found. So at this moment, be KIND TO YOURSELF. Spend time with yourself every day. Ask: "How am I really feeling?" Be totally honest and describe your feelings to yourself. Don't whitewash them, but just describe what they are. Confused, dead, empty, unattractive, relieved, stunned, tired, hopeful or in pain - whatever - just name them. Trauma-bonded people spend a lot of time suppressing their feelings, so now is the time to look at them and see what is really your feeling and what that feeling actually is. Try this: think of a really happy moment in your life, unconnected with that narcissist. Then, something very unhappy, also preferably not to do with them. On a scale between those two, ask, where are you in this present moment? You might protest that this is a bit hard, in other words, not kind to yourself. It is kind: you are giving yourself attention! It's a bit like going to a doctor. You're not well, you know, and your health was neglected. Remember: "Kindness isn't blindness."

Rest. Can you manage to start work a bit later, or choose not to take on something right now? We don't all have the luxury, but if you do, take it. The actual fact of working is good for you, but you are not going to help yourself if you overdo it. Sleep enough. You may be someone who hasn't been sleeping well, you may have been living on tenterhooks with stress caused by your abuser, and so on. Try to eat well and exercise moderately, and don't try sleeping-tablets unless you really have to, or drink alcohol for the sake of sleeping. This is the best but weirdest advice to people who can't sleep well: don't worry about it. The only way to sleep is NOT to try!! Sorry, that sounds awful. Yet sleep is a process of letting go, and you can't force it. Don't you remember the night before going away on a holiday you were looking forward to? Or before a hospital operation? So don't try: don't go to bed early, go late. Think to yourself that you've managed with the sleep you've had, so that your situation can't be that bad regarding sleep. Better sleeping habits will catch you up later, on the sly!

Do pleasant, relaxing things. If you can afford a head-and-neck massage, get one. Or go to a sauna. Or just walk if it's good weather: some of the best things are free. Working out in a gym helps you to feel good afterwards - just don't strain too much at this time. Try aromatherapy or breathing exercises. Use vitamin and other supplements wisely, getting medical advice if unsure. Stress can do bad things to your brain and nervous system, and things like Vitamins B, E or D, Omega compounds in fish and other oils, can have a beneficial effect on our brains. Have a good meal in the sort of place you DIDN'T go to when you were with your narcissist (in other words, if he disdained diners: go to an old-fashioned diner... or if he was so mean that he called good restaurants "catering-thieves": go to a good restaurant). Eat healthy food at home - and not too much junk food. As we pointed out, you risk getting into an addiction-cycle with enjoying junk food, then feeling awful afterwards when you suffer indigestion, blood-pressure changes, and shame. Don't feel ashamed; pamper yourself with healthy activities instead! Relaxation videos or audio-tracks can help most people to feel unstressed. If you drink alcoholic drinks, it is best to do so only in company, and in moderation. When you can be with friends or any good people, then it's OK to drink; only in moderation, so that the next morning you DON'T feel bad. Hangovers only make you feel guilty! Drinking on your own is not normally recommended for anyone. If you are very isolated, then go to a restaurant and have a beer or a glass of wine there, not at home. And do enjoy the meal!

This is all about un-learning what your abuser taught you, which was to punish yourself for his or her sake. You are also disciplining your mind and body, and you have a right to be happy while doing so.

A skill that recovering addicts (in other words, you!) need to learn is to INTERRUPT YOUR PATTERNS. You see, you'll have a lot of bad habits of thought and behavior bashed into you by your trauma. You need to break them. For example: someone is feeling really bad. She's cried and cried for hours that day. Later on she feels like crying again, but says to herself that this is just too much. So she must watch a comedy she likes! Or to give another example: a man feels so bad on waking that he just wants to stay in bed. No - he should get up and do the opposite: take a walk or go for a run.

Be PREPARED. In the majority of cases, a narcissistic sociopath is going to try to get back into your life, if you were the one who left. Even if it was you who were 'dumped', there is still the type, for example, who sends nasty messages from the home he shares with his next victim, threatening not to pay his son's school fees unless the son writes him a letter. This is when you must strive to have no contact with him. Block his number on your 'phone; don't follow him on social media, and take off anything that showed you and your abuser together - it's an embarrassment now. Don't reply to anything he sends. If you can't change your e-mail, then what comes from him, don't read. If your son simply must write that letter... then tell him to do it in the most cool, factual way he can. No insults, no revenge, no personal warmth at all. Just write - and giving away no facts that the abuser might use against either of you. You need to be INDIFFERENT, and to look that way.

DON'T go back to the narcissist! Even if you think you might run out of money, and wonder if being beaten is the price you'll have to pay - No!! By the way, on the topic of being kind to yourself: if you did return to your abuser, only to be abused again, and now you've left once more... forgive yourself! It was crazy, but you were an addict. Being firm but kind to yourself, is the way to move forward, and to overcome the temptation to return. Temptation doesn't go away when the opposite is distorted to look like punishing yourself; it will lessen when you are protecting yourself and becoming happy again.

Don't blame yourself. Your sense of self-worth needs some care. Think about this, to be mindful and kind to yourself at the same time: if your self-worth could have been damaged so quickly by someone who is sick in the head, then it can't have been really solid to begin with! That isn't a criticism of you, but it's an acknowledgement of reality. You were a vulnerable person whom the narcissist picked to use. The way to see it now is not to lament how your self-esteem has been shredded, but to see this break with your toxic relationship, and these exercises in mindful awareness of your emotions and thinking, as an opportunity to build it again. In fact, to build it up to something better than it has ever been before. That isn't to turn you into a braggart or a wind-bag! Such people don't have a solid self-esteem at all. Don't be afraid of wanting healthy self-esteem.

You need information to help you to detach yourself from the narcissist: to help you to realize who and what a narcissist is. This is not just that you might understand what he or she was doing to you - and that is very, very important for healing and strengthening yourself - but in order that you can identify and avoid narcissists of any type in the future. Traumatized people have a tendency to attract manipulators, even more than once. To say what has just been asserted is not to try to make you paranoid: when you are stronger, freer and healthier inside, you will be much less vulnerable to narcissists and therefore far less likely to find them attractive or "friendly-looking". You will not be afraid of them in the sense of feeling that you are always in danger of falling into their clutches, sensing that they still have power over you. However, you will fear them (if you see what we mean here) in the way you would fear a skunk when you saw one! Keep reading good self-help articles, and if you have mental exercises given to you by a counselor or therapist, do them thoroughly.

On that subject: get yourself support! Society hasn't recognized the seriousness of narcissistic abuse until recently, and people have yet to understand generally that it is as much of an addiction and a condition, as is the abuse of drugs. People who support you can remind you of why you made the decision to get out of a toxic relationship, and did. Other people can stand with you when you are tempted to go back to an abusive relationship, and motivate you not to; when you feel really, really desolated, they can comfort you and give you hope to go on and embrace a much better future.

You would do well to have professional counseling; if at all possible, by people who have experience in healing from narcissistic abuse. What you are doing is like getting off drugs. So many people, especially men, think that they can and have to "do it all by myself". There is a lack of humility, a lack of realism, and the danger of ending up in a worse state, with this attitude. Sorry, we have to say this. If you don't acknowledge that you need help, you just fool yourself. Remember the first step of Alcoholics Anonymous requires them to admit that God, however they understood Him to be, was the one who could help them, and that without a higher power they could not help themselves! We have to admit that the words we use can be confusing, so here we must explain... You may have heard us telling you to stand on your own feet in the stages of recovery later on, that you and you alone can make the final decisions. This is not to say that anyone can do it ALL by himself or herself. In this way you are not different! All the other people needed help to change the things deep inside them, even though, after getting help, they had to do the bit that they, and they alone, could do. This is what we mean.

Help can also be from an abuse-support group. This support could be a group of people who meet locally; it could also be a group that meets online, anonymously perhaps, from anywhere in the world; or on social media, or a newsletter. Such groups can benefit from having a professional counselor or therapist involved. They can help you to feel oriented when your circumstances are new and confusing, and abuse seems so dangerously familiar. Don't go back! Don't go back! It'll be worse for you if you do... You can also ask advice from an older and wiser acquaintance you can confide in, such as a teacher you had years ago at school; a minister of religion, a trusted family-member. Doctors can help, and in some cases they may decide, for example, that someone who has co-morbid PTSD (i.e. has other problems plus trauma) will need a course of medication to help them in this time. We don't recommend anti-depressants unless a medical practitioner thinks it's necessary. Your mind needs conscious care, and your body, and you need to work on your emotions. Medication isn't a short-cut.

You have to be healed of the wounds abusers cause, to protect your own self. So, again, you need to see what damage happened to you in your own life, from the abuser who you had a relationship with. Probably, you are going to realize that parts of your relationship were never genuine, that there was a lot of hiding, a lot of sham. You'll need to come to terms with that. It will be painful to understand that what you were living, the intoxicating times and the abused times, was never a real relationship. You need to do this to separate yourself from the narcissist, and the 'spirit of narcissism', you can say, that you don't continue to attract these types.

When you read about abusive relationships, you'll see again and again how narcissists work on other people. Interestingly, some of the self-proclaimed 'pick-up artists' say openly - "If you want a girl, take her on a roller-coaster ride." Before even the cycle of abuse starts, narcissistic types cultivate a sense of there being some kind of danger or excitement, and yet safety as well. They start making victims identify them with safety and reward. When they begin to distance themselves and grow cold and hostile, the sense of danger grows; and then when they become sweet and charming again, even though THEY were the source of danger, something within a susceptible victim sees this as being rescue and safety.

In the 'honeymoon period' abusers encourage their prey to be open about their plans and aspirations. It's very human to want to talk about these things, if anyone seems interested. They will talk about what seem to be common interests, perhaps even seeming to tell you their problems. It doesn't really matter if these are truly their interests and their problems, or if they tell a load of lies. The fact is, they are getting you to talk. Not only is your sympathy being attracted, but they are getting information about you. That's going to be used to use you... Without doubt, they may be saying a lot, but you can be sure that they are always hiding as much and more from you, as they tell. Even before the charming period started, they were probably planning to try using you. As said, sociopaths are good at spotting traumatized people. They may see your head held down, your moods expressed in your face, or recognize your vulnerability from the things you say. If they see what they want, they approach you. As you open up, your deep emotions will show, and they will see them.

Think back about those deep, powerful feelings that came up soon after you met that sociopath. Either how he or she tried to make you feel, or the old, lifelong feelings you found it hard to keep down. Think: did those feelings not take you back to your childhood? Did they make you think of parents' neglect? Or were you brought up with a parent or parents who practised 'splitting'? This is a word used to describe caregivers who reward a child for "good" behavior (as they see it) with attention and "discard" or punish what they don't like by ignoring and, or, criticizing the child totally. Love and attention become conditional. This is the place where your deepest and oldest hurts are, and though the narcissist comes along later, their behavior will make use of it.

Generally, victims are people who can feel for other people, in other words, empathetic; but what they start doing soon after meeting a narcissistic victimizer is taking their own empathy, giving themselves no attention with it, and devoting their empathy to the narcissist.

No doubt you have expectations of other people, but you have to understand what you ended up thinking in relation to your abuser. Expectations often get in the way of happiness! We know that can be so (haven't we all ended up disappointing someone whose expectations of us were unreasonable and actually selfish?) Yet victims expect the unreasonable: for example, that their abuser will feel true regret for what he or she's done. A highly narcissistic character? Highly unlikely! Other victims think that their abuser will automatically reap the consequences of what he or she sowed, and that this will lead to their changing... if that victim just waits... No! Why must things happen just because you wait for them? Finally, other victims again are angry, no doubt with reason, but in their rage they want to see their abusers punished and destroyed by the consequences of their actions. This isn't healthy. To say that is not to deny the evil they do - it is to know the truth that wishing ill on someone else is not going to bring you any good. It leads to bitterness and will rob you of peace.

We have just told you to read books, watch videos and talk to people who can educate you about abusive relationships. This may sound odd to add, but we have to warn you: DON'T FALL INTO THE TRAP OF BECOMING A NARCISSISM-INFORMATION JUNKIE!! The reason you are learning about this stuff is because you need to DO something with what you know: heal yourself, protect yourself, become less vulnerable to these people, and just become the person you were created to be! It's the "paralysis of analysis" if you become fixated on getting information that takes your mind off the pain; instead you have to get the information to tackle that pain.

When you are in recovery, you may find that there is someone else in your life, or some other people, who are not evil, not narcissists, not the person who abused you, but who are still not good for you in this state. Maybe they are just needy people, maybe just burdensome, maybe just don't understand you. It isn't wrong to tell yourself - or them - that you just need time to heal yourself, to concentrate on recovering your life, and that you don't have a lot of energy for other things at this time. If they worry you with their obsessions or their plans or why the celebrities hate X... you need to shut out this noise from your mind. It's not being selfish to look after yourself, to give yourself space, after trauma.

Finally, why not cultivate spirituality? Many victims had a sort of awakening deep inside, a moment when they just saw that they had to leave their abusers. Or some highly-unpleasant co-incidence happened to them when they made up their minds to leave, as if something invisible and bad was trying to stop them. This would not be a reason to give up, but to hope and persevere! Prayer and meditation gives us an explanation for otherwise mysterious things, and provides those who practise them with the ability to see the opportunities hiding in otherwise tragic events. You can say to yourself, "There were lessons I had to learn, and this has taught me what I wouldn't have appreciated if this hadn't happened." Spirituality also helps people to become more in control of their thoughts and actions, more at peace and more joyful.

Chapter 19
Why You Have to Go 'No Contact' to Break the Trauma Bond

When learning about breaking trauma bonds, the reader will often see the words, 'No Contact'. What this refers to is more or less a 'detox' regimen to recover from the experience of a traumatic, toxic relationship. It's the relationship-version of 'rehab' for alcoholics and drug-dependents. There are other exercises a recovering victim can do, but this is something all abused people need to follow.

It's also like quitting smoking! Quite simply, you have to quit ONE HUNDRED PERCENT...

Have you heard people saying the following?

"I'll stop smoking when I'm older - I'm still young and healthy."
"I can just cut it down: I don't have to stop altogether."
"I'm having too much stress at the moment. Yes, I want to do it, but now's not a good time."
"When I'm ready to stop, I'll know."
"I'm too old to change a habit of forty years!"
"But I exercise, and I don't eat fatty foods..."
"My grandfather lived to ninety, and he smoked till the end."
"When I stop, I go crazy. I turn into an ogre. My children would leave home! It's just not possible for me."
"Think of all the taxes we smokers pay. That all goes to the government, so we are benefiting the country in our own way."
"When I think of life without it, and that awful craving... life will never be the same again. Just sort of... colorless."

The excuses grow stranger and stranger. Yes, all those smokers are talking ADDICT talk! They forget that the habit is expensive, only really enjoyable for the first few puffs, forces you to keep going outside for smoke breaks, kills your senses of smell and taste, has been implicated by the medical profession to be among the causes of many diseases, and makes you feel BAD when you can't light up. No cigarettes at five in the morning? You can buy them only from seven onward... Torture is light compared to those two hours!

We aren't really talking about smoking in this book. However, if you've given up already, that's a learning experience for giving up a toxic relationship; if you haven't quit, we definitely advise it, perhaps once you are in a 'survivor' stage of healing from addiction to a person. Then, re-read and just remember those excuses in the paragraph above...

The excuses some emotionally-abused victims make are as sad, as irrational and as stubborn as those. And like those, they just aren't true! In this chapter and the following ones, we have to drive home some vitally-important, but hard facts. This is for your inner good. Like a bird staring helplessly at a snake about to strike it, victims sometimes waver and agonize about what to do when they are in real danger: physically - perhaps - emotionally and physiologically, always.

Such as, "I'll just keep contact with him by 'phone while the children are of school-age."
"I don't care if I see him every month or so. In that way, he won't get too angry with me."
"It's going to be hard. I think I'd go crazy if I left now. I'll wait till New Year."
"I'll know inside when I'm ready to leave her."
"To remember those first couple of months we had together, and some of the holidays we've had, keeps me going. I could never just forget him and not see him ever again."
"I really should leave him. But I'm so scared of not managing on my own, you see."
"I don't have the willpower to stop worrying about him. I feel better when I know how he is, though I won't actually go to see him."

Do you recognize yourself? We have to urge you... you aren't going to get better until you stop this drug! When addicts talk like this, they are blind to the damage they've suffered. Trauma-bond detoxing is a difficult experience, but the results are worth it! The same chemicals that cause chaos in the brains of Stockholm Syndrome hostages, alcoholics and nicotine slaves, are coursing through your veins...

Those symptoms will start to go once your contact with the abuser has gone. So...

You are going to block off all contact with the narcissist. Not distance yourself, not give yourself more space. It may take several different steps, but if you can do the whole lot quickly, so much the better! Block his phone number. His e-mail address. Block him on social media; stop looking at anything he features on. Delete photographs you appear in together. Don't call him, send a letter or send him any communication at all. Don't go near where he lives, and don't contact his friends or family. The only way to be free of the chemical-conditioning in your brain is to stop stimulating it, and he is the stimulus. (In the case of a female narcissist, put 'she' where we have 'he'. It's just the same).

If you think there would be no harm in talking to your abuser's cousin (who's really quite friendly, most unlike the abuser these days; but who mentions that abuser, just to fill you in, to 'help' you...) then you are totally wrong. Just hearing about your abuser from their cousin would give you a surge of feeling - a twinge of pain, an unpleasant memory, or a fuzzy warm memory of how it felt when it was good - and that is a drug reaction! All of the memories of an abuser after narcissistic maltreatment are stressful and lack peace, and so you need to stop provoking them. Stress makes stress hormones... Social media are a big problem if you don't restrict yourself: you might see an 'ex' with someone else and feel thrown away; you might end up seeing the stuff that person says and does to look miserable on his profile picture, to try to make you feel sorry. It's all trying to hook you back to the see-saw of feelings that got you into an addicted state. If people who know both of you can respect your decision to cut all ties with your abuser, and therefore not give you any news about them - let alone tell them anything about YOU, God forbid! - then you can continue to talk to them, if they are people who are good to you. Even in this case, you might want to cut down on speaking to them for a while, if their very identity just reminds you of your abuser so much. It can be handled kindly with just a quick reason: that you need time to heal, to spend some time by yourself. Good people should understand. If mutual acquaintances don't respect this need of yours for no news of your abuser or contact made, then avoid them. Those acquaintances are not true friends, are they? Friends would respect your will. So: cut the rot out. When you look back on this, the more sudden and total your break was, the better you will feel about the way you did it.

Narcissists can be handled best not by anger and threats (they are driven to retaliate); not by passive surrender (they just take more and more from their victims); and not by patiently explaining to them why what they have done is wrong (they just ignore it); they are handled best when you, who were the victim, are INDIFFERENT!

Cool, calm and collected people can't give the narcissist his or her knowledge of their weak points, because they don't lose their calm. Talking to the abuser, even light chatter, risks giving away facts about yourself or your situation. To know that abusers literally live by weakening, disturbing and overpowering their prey, is to know that you have to behave in the opposite way - strong, calm, stable, and silent. By nature they are hideously competitive: their relationships are endless competitions where they pit themselves against their partner in love, business, or what you will - and rig every contest into something they can win. This makes them play mind-games of "tit-for-tat", of "point-scoring", and "one-better-than-you". So rather than try to retaliate (because if you 'win', narcissist fumes with rage, and starts competing harder...), just STOP PLAYING. That means, having no contact.

At this point we return to remember the person reading this book who is not a victim, but who is trying to help from the outside. If you have the victim's trust and agreement, you too must try to keep the abuser away from them. No doubt you will be more than willing to do so, but the last-made points about calm indifference and the personality of a narcissist, apply to you too. You see, your natural, protective instincts are very likely to make you want to retaliate against the abuser. Given that some abusers are quite dangerous to anyone, and highly unpleasant at any rate, you have to make sure that you aren't just provoking him or her to gratify your own desire for punishment. We're not saying, just give up and wave a white flag - no - but we are saying that your action must be as firm and as quick as possible. You, too, should try to make no attempt to communicate with your loved one's abuser. If you have to, to take the pressure off them, you too must be as unemotional and to-the-point as you can. You almost want to make the abuser seem of no importance to you, either. This is to protect your loved one's peace of mind, and prevent an enraged sociopath from trying all the harder to disturb them.

What does a victim do, whose abuser is trying deliberately to stalk her - or him? We cannot give professional legal advice here, but this would seem to be a case of getting a 'restraining order' or other such legal prohibition against a former spouse, for example, from going near the area where the ex-partner lives. Where some communication has to occur for legal reasons - such as the process of a divorce, for example - then it must be with a go-between, the lawyer in this case. In that way, a lot of the emotional stress is taken away, and you don't have to see or hear your abuser in person, or receive all his or her communications yourself.

If you are a recovering victim, you want to start cultivating a mindset that can put the past behind you, can be almost indifferent about it. This is so that you can look to the future more. Being at peace will help you to achieve forgiveness, when the time comes. Hearing the word, 'forgiveness' - after such denunciations as we have made of abusers, and of the temptation to cling to them - you might wonder why we would bother with it. The fact is that as you heal, you will start to feel a lot of anger with your abuser as you accept the fact of what happened to you. However, anger and bitterness do not help anyone to heal, or to distance themselves from memories of a person or incident. You will need to let go of anger and bitterness to be happy. This is forgiveness.

Forgiveness is just that - forgiveness. It does not imply becoming friendly again with a sociopath, starting to talk to them again, etc. You will continue, and be quite at peace with having, NO CONTACT. You will have no wish for the 'excitement' of a fight. That excitement is a drug-high that will be followed inevitably by a drug-low. You want neither extreme. You have to be firm and calm, and carry on healing.

Chapter 20
Detoxing After a Trauma Bond

T o help you to understand the way you feel after leaving a traumatic relationship, we could compare it to going into a "rehabilitation clinic", that is, 'rehab'. Just like those people, you have committed yourself by free will to be helped to break free from an addiction. Deep down, you knew that the addiction was wrecking your life. You were bold and brave enough to take the plunge, and now you've done it.

Unfortunately, soon after the newness and relief you feel right at the beginning, there are, just as with 'rehab', withdrawal symptoms. Therapists these days are telling newly-recovering victims that what they have to do is as bad as, almost the same as, coming off a mind-affecting drug. This is not said to frighten you, but to help you to understand the state your brain was in, and the work that must be done to go through to achieve freedom and normal, healthy thought-patterns. The withdrawal symptoms may come on very quickly, and are deeply unpleasant.

The reactions are totally irrational. It might make sense that there was some bond because of life shared during a certain time, the 'honeymoon-period' memories, or the very real fact of having children together. Yet these are not the reason: for in a case where there are no children, and there were few times of the abuser's being charming, victims of a trauma bond still grieve and feel disturbed when they leave a relationship, to the point of wanting to go back. They can even say that they see their partner at that moment and no longer love him or her - yet still want to return!

It's addiction. Part emotional, part bodily and part chemical. Your abuser is also addicted to the supply of attention that he or she got out of you! We have explained that 'Narcs' are, as it were, cold and dead on the inside, and literally suck the life out of you in order to live by the pleasure of taking. They have, in a sense, taken your soul or inner life captive. Something inside you both animal (preservation instinct... fawning) and spiritual (pleading for them to be merciful and just to you, to "do the right thing in conscience") tries to protect you, but they've got hold of it, used it, and actually trapped you.

It's eerie: the more you would try to change a 'Narc', the more he or she would try to use you, and would change YOU - for the worse, till you'd be emptied out and dead!

Doesn't the old saying go, "God helps those who help themselves"? Leave that person in God's hands, if you can see it that way. Instead, you have to become the change you want to see. You are the part of the situation that you are responsible for; and if there's anyone who can change a narcissist - highly unlikely - it's not you, their victim.

In your brokenness and trauma, you must free yourself from any toxic relationship with any person, any use of a substance which enslaves you, and any habit that you are trapped in. The solution's the same, and it is inside you. You tried to get approval and love as a small child, and didn't, or failed to get enough to be at peace. You looked for it in another person, and ended up with your abuser, trying to get from them what you didn't from your childhood caregiver. It's as if you re-lived it, tried to plead and argue and love them as they were in the past, in the person you were bonded to recently! Possibly, one of your parents was a victim then as you are now, so you just learned "victimhood" from the cradle.

You need to set up your own voice in the world: your own beliefs, your own values, and practise making your own decisions. You will be happier when you accept that you have the right to do so, that you are made with enough goodness in you to be able to give love to others because you have a healthy love of self. You won't be having love stolen from you in such a way that it makes (fakes?) it seem that you are giving real love, when you are really shouting a heartfelt cry for love to be given to you, that fell on cold, uncaring ears...

Anxiety and certain kinds of depression follow from feeling as you do. Realize that what you have always thought of as 'normal' was this anxiety and depression, and it isn't normal. We are not saying that no-body ever feels anxiety, but the constant levels in the background that dogged you through life are not reactions to day-to-day stresses, and they don't help you to avoid danger. Then you ended up with depression from an abusive relationship or relationships on top of that!

Be positive: you can feel better; more normal. You can learn.

When you feel that you are bad, you begin to treat yourself badly. You eat badly, use alcohol or chemical substances that affect you badly, maybe even throw yourself at anyone who seems attractive, for a bit of happy feeling, and put up with being used and thrown away because you feel like rubbish. It's another vicious circle: after doing these things, you WILL feel like garbage!! Different addictions can include watching every crime-channel on the television, somehow seeing relief at discovering that the twisted minds of the criminals featured there are worse than your 'rubbish' as you see it; or maybe you become morbidly curious about all the wrongdoings in your neighborhood, and start gossiping, somehow making yourself feel better than the people you spread stories about... and afterwards, feel dirty and sad.

Your body has been hooked on the chemicals that it makes when you feel strong emotions. All of those chemicals made by all of those emotions (not just the pleasurable ones) are potentially addictive when there is a twist of background and circumstances. The effect on the body is considerable, and it's BAD.

When you can face your negative emotions and the flashbacks caused by withdrawal in a structured, calm way, with a therapist there to guide you; and then on your own but following their guidelines, you can start to break the cycle of addiction. As it was mentioned earlier, a victim's mind has a critical voice that has been there since childhood - powerfully added to by the deliberate criticism and hostility of their abuser. Silencing that voice is a process of reminding oneself of the lies and distortions it tells; that your abuse was real and not imagined; that love does not need to be earned; that the opinions of a malignant narcissist are of no use or relevance to his or her victim. You will need to be aware

144

of this negativity, and to spend time resisting it, counteracting it with the truth, above all the truth that IT WASN'T MY FAULT. How can you think that you are useless, if you realize that your abuser chose you... because you were, in a bad way, useful to him or to her? You contained goodness they preyed on! You need to find ways to put your abilities into practice, but without fear or any need to apologize for yourself.

Flashbacks need to be examined, instead of pushed away. You'll ask: What am I remembering? What exactly happened? How did I feel at that moment? What could I have done then, and if nothing, how can I act positively about this feeling now? If I could have done something then but didn't, how can I learn from this in the present? Is it time to look at my future in this matter, instead? In this type of exercise, you are looking at the "fact of your emotions" and once identifying them, you judge them. Always, you need to remind yourself that you are a survivor: you are looking at memories of the past, and you can and should act in the present so as to choose not to let the past define who you are.

Reflecting on the FACTS came up at the beginning of this book, when we presented ways to judge whether or not you are in a trauma bond, even whether or not you are being abused. What are the unarguable truths of your situation? What incidents can you remember? Is there a particular reason for my feeling so afraid or inadequate? How was I being confused deliberately by my abuser, and once I realize that, what can I begin to explain? Also, you may start to see things from your childhood in a new light when you recall them carefully. "Wow, that was unfair!" you may say. Or, "So she said that because she hated my father", and so on. Don't give your abuser or abusers the "benefit of the doubt" here, but decide what the evidence suggests you should think about their actions and words. This is where a therapist or other outside person can help you to see things from another person's point of view. That's all part of seeing the facts. Knowledge is power!

Looking after your body is as important here as is caring for your mind: when you eat, sleep, relax and exercise, the body will start to repair the effects of the bad chemicals it has generated, and this will, in turn, affect your moods for the better.

Chapter 21
Detoxing - Cold Turkey (with Wasabi Sauce!)

A ll along throughout this book, we have been encouraging victims of any kind of abuse to take control of their lives, and to break free from narcissistic manipulators, liars and destroyers. We have repeated the message that such freedom is necessary for them to start living again, to recover from serious mental, physical and emotional damage, and avoid further trauma. We haven't tried to avoid telling victims that this is going to be difficult, and have explained why it certainly will be. Instead, we've given every encouragement to you, if you are being victimized or trying to recover after abuse, to persevere.

Some victims may still be hesitating. They might still be deciding if they can cope with the shock of change; or, are they desperately trying to convince themselves that a handsome, clever man with amazing talents, but hideously cruel - or a beautiful, educated woman, but with a vindictive, selfish streak - must have some redeeming quality, and that they can never find anyone like them again? And this, when that person has literally ruined their lives!

Others may feel so awful after the break-up, that they wonder how they will ever think clearly again. They may have been treated so badly that they suffer disturbing flash-backs and nightmares (the classic PTSD), and yet they feel forced, deep inside, to say that they love that abuser.

Are you any one of these? Human nature is both amazing and frustrating. We have a tendency to handle ourselves very badly: just when we need to be gentle with ourselves, we are harsh - and the other way around! At several places in earlier chapters, we have showed you how and when to be kind to yourself after trauma.

Yet some victims wallow in trauma!

What follows is going to be deliberately forceful. It is meant for those who - despite truly horrible circumstances - just sigh, and whine, "But I can't bring myself to do what I read. How can they expect me to do that when I feel the way I do? Why don't they understand that I can't just walk away from that person/walk away from what I've gone through?"

The experiences of millions of recovered victims say that you can. You have to go "Cold Turkey"! You'll need help, and in the case of someone who is still clinging mentally to his or her abuser, that help has to be rather strong. A bit like wasabi sauce (hot radish). But it'll help you to chomp your way through the 'cold turkey'! So read on!

DETOXING BY EXPOSURE TO YOUR EMOTIONS

The abuser did vile things to you. For example: stole, spread lies about you, slept around - all of these on multiple occasions - and then left you. Actually, for many people, especially when they begin to feel a proper anger with a narcissist, there is a sense of hurt pride. "How could I have let this happen to me?"; "Why didn't I protect myself?"; "Can blood-suckers just take the life out of me?" people will ask themselves. Such questioning can lead to bitterness. Coupled with shame, which socio-paths who abuse are good at provoking, bitterness can be very un-healthy. Such traumatized victims can become aggressive, anti-social and self-destructive. The targets of this aggression are, sadly, most likely to be the ones who are closest to them!

It goes back to the cycle of narcissistic abuse. They throw you down into the mud, then pick you up again. Somehow, the human mind sees this 'picking me up out of the mud' as rescue, and tries to make you feel grateful, pitifully... The other side of your mind sees the way you've needed help, and not been able to stand on your own two feet, as hu-miliating. So you feel shame, hate yourself, and think you love your abuser. That is the twisted power of narcissists; power being their ob-session.

So it's time to escape! Your emotions are in a state, and you need to work on them. That will actually be harder than it seems, because you are going to have to work on ALL of them; including the irrational, the dark, and the confusing feelings you have.

Some of what is going to be covered in this mental exercise is uncomfortable. Yet it has to be dealt with, and we don't want to hide anything from you, precisely because our purpose is to help. You have to start taking responsibility for your emotions. Some counselors have seen that victims who are so mature in many ways, become almost adolescent when talking about their abusers. They describe love-bombing in almost teenage ways, like a 'crush'; recall arguments that sound like youngsters fighting over who is guilty of breaking a window; agonize over small injustices, and seem indifferent to great ones. Victims may start planning petty retaliations, sound as if they want to win the next game in a series... Dear victim - wouldn't you rather get on with your life?

OK, so some of your emotions are quite irrational. This has been pointed out, and explained. It wasn't your fault. However, now you need to sort them out and be responsive, not merely reactive. Accept everything you did and everything you felt, the fact of it. Accept that you are out of the toxic relationship, and ask yourself how you feel now. Inevitably, always, there is sadness. You need to accept that grief and grow by accepting it. You absolutely must not avoid painful emotions; and if you have to repeat things to yourself, write things about yourself, perhaps go to sessions with a therapist, you will have to do what you are advised to, to get the benefit. In matters of personal growth, the problem is inside you, and it is in there that you'll need to look.

You cannot blame incidental facts, circumstances and small quirks of character that you and your abuser did, or didn't share. It's not because you didn't get that job and he was disappointed in you... it's because you were taken in, wounded and post-traumatic as you were, by a sociopathic predator who told you a sad story, maybe, and when you reacted with sympathy, he or she knew there was a sucker to take prisoner! That sad story brought forth a painful memory for you, of your own inner child, and the narcissist actually put himself or herself in the place of your inner child whom you feel sorry for... You'll be made to think that if you rescue Mr. Weirdloved, you are rescuing yourself as well. You can't rescue him... you need to mature from thinking that you could.

Or, have your obsessions with your abuser turned from love to hate? That might get you out of his house, but it won't get him out of your head. You need to stop obsessing and let go. Or did you try and try to give him more and more love, believing that it had to change the way he was, if you could but give enough? Were you flattering yourself that you were the only one in the world who could save him? That was nonsense... You need to let go of it, as much as of him. Just like every other trauma-bonded victim in the world had to, has to and will have to... It's quite simple, uncomfortably so.

You will need to expose yourself to the horrible flashbacks and nightmares of your abuse, and those of your childhood hurts - yes, with patience, guidance - and face them. Then you will start to heal, when you don't try to run away from them. Many victims don't get out of their victim-mentality to become survivors, because it's hard and a little bit humiliating. They complain about their lives and become defensive when told that they will need to stop complaining, and accept what they have to do. You see... is anything that is worthwhile done quite so easily? And it will be worthwhile!

A PTSD exposure therapy, combined with a willingness to feel all your raw emotions including the ugliest ones, is an effective way to stop flashbacks, whether from your childhood or your recent abuse. It's hard stuff, but can be done with the help of a therapist, and a structure, and a willingness to get to the bottom of how to stop feeling the way you do. Can you not see that a trauma bond happens to people who are frightened of life? That fear kept you bound to your abuser; now you can embrace life - and to do so you will have to face up to life. Life can be hard, but it's real. What will waste your time and life, and that of anyone who is in your support-group, is trying to fool yourself.

149

If you want one person out of your head, follow the steps: it may become dull, may become painful, may even become boring - but you must do it, to get the results. It sounds a bit like gym work!! Suffering is part of life, and your abuser - who made you suffer so - was LYING when he or she made you think they could take you to a place where there was no pain, when they buttered you up with fake love. Yet once you've decided that the abuser is not getting any more of your precious life to waste, you will suffer far less in the end; than if you let that person have the attention he or she wants, and all you get is a false feeling of having given to a fake charity!

Either on your own, or in the presence of someone who is counseling you, you will remember and visualize the worst experiences you had of abuse. It will make you feel bad... but, when that happens, you will tell yourself what was being done to you, accept that it was indeed abuse, and use your reason to understand that what was done to you was evil. When you remember your helpless feelings, for example as you were hit, you will also repeat to yourself that now, you are not helpless. You have left your abuser and you are busy healing your life. If you remember how you apologized for some supposed error (going out in the car to see your great-aunt, without telling him), and pleaded with your abuser, feeling a sort of desperation that he would see that you loved him... you will recall that this same desperation, even as you feel it again, was the result of a cruel trick to make you obey him! You'll use your reason to remind yourself that your abuser is not worthy of respect.

These mental exercises will be exhausting at first, but you will feel better afterwards. As you do them again and again, you will feel less and less of the power of your memories. This method is being used by many ex-servicemen and women who were 'shell-shocked' by their experiences of war, and it can be and is being adapted to serve the victims of abusive relationships.

Chapter 22
Dating Again After the Trauma Bond

I n the first stages of leaving a toxic relationship, and especially after getting away from an abusive narcissist, you, the victim, just have to look after yourself. It's a little like being in Intensive Care, or at any rate in hospital, for your mind and heart.

Once you are living a new and freer life, and can start to think of the future properly, the question might start coming into your mind: "Am I going to meet someone new?" Or you might wonder if Mr. Right/ Miss Right will ever find you. Part of you may feel desperately lonely, and crave company and romance - the other half of you probably feels decidedly uncomfortable and afraid. "Once bitten, twice shy"!

So: in the first stages of recovery, you definitely don't want to start dating anyone. We spoke about the danger an unhealed person has of being sucked in by another 'Narc', or just getting into emotional confusion and hurt, from an attempt to reach out to someone who turns out not to be compatible. Take your time.

By now, we are dealing with further stages on the road to recovery. This is when you can think, and you will think, about connecting with good people for friendship, family... and romance.

When will you be ready? There can be no artificial, rigid rule. You'll know! Sorry, that sounds so lazy, but it's not. The fact that you have started thinking about meeting someone is one clue that you are moving forward.

"But what about memories, emotions suddenly flaring up, those dreaded flashbacks?" we hear you objecting. This is something to consider calmly and using reason. There is a fact: our brains remember things. Intense things (read, trauma) are highly memorable. It doesn't matter if you were in a trauma-bond relationship one year ago or twenty years ago: you will remember it!

Techniques to expose yourself to the memories with guided help, to work through them in a controlled way, to use reason to look after your emotions, will take the power out of them. We've said this already. Avoiding a stimulus in a situation does not help you to deal with it positively... Avoidance isn't going to make you a stronger person, or enable you to be intimate again. In a new interaction with someone, that might become romantic, you will have to keep going with this process, always reminding yourself that this is someone ELSE, not your 'ex', and in any case, you are now more adept at spotting a 'Narc' and keeping him or her away.

So, there's no reason to procrastinate only because of your bad memories. Yes, there will be bad memories, but until you deal with them, they won't diminish. And this is the important insight - dating again can take your attention off your trauma, and be a very healthy way to start living more freely! Ask yourself: "What am I looking for? Who am I looking for?" Maybe just to feel attractive again; maybe just to have a laugh. Maybe just to enjoy life without spending every waking moment planning mountainous issues and dread-serious plans!

One of the side-effects of trauma is the way it makes you sad and serious. Add into that a narcissist, who consumes and sucks up all of your time, all of your energy. That isn't normal or healthy. To live again is to be able to let some things just flow by, and to savor the present moment. You were almost brainwashed in your abuse to think that love is a lie, romance is **** by another name, that the world and everyone in it is rotten. Well, you know that isn't so. There is a lot of bad in the world, but it's still a beautiful world, and there's still beauty and goodness in people. Romance is still possible...

Being realistic, you acknowledge that when you do start to feel romantic, to sense attraction to someone again, you will feel some anxiety.

This is to be expected. You were programmed by your abuser to stress; and if you go on a date one evening, and hear nothing from the new acquaintance the next day, you may be reminded of the "cold shoulder" treatment you had from your 'Narc' seesawing away from his or her 'love-bombing' the day before. You need to be calm, and practice the awareness of your emotions that was described in previous chapters.

Ask yourself: "What do I want out of dating?" Try to be clear about your goals. Maybe finding your husband or wife for life is a goal, but that's long-term. In the short-term, perhaps it is to learn how to be open, how to meet people again, and no more. Relationship counselors will advise you to take things easy at this point. That doesn't mean using the person you date, saying, "Hi, and goodbye!", let alone any kind of one-night-stand (that last one would mess up your emotions and memories totally...). It just means, taking time to enjoy dating in itself, without frantic expectations.

Your trauma-bonded past relationship or relationships were times of serious, deep emotions and shocking intensity. Your whole being was pulled into the vortex. Now you've just been engaged in the critical, life-saving task of healing yourself and getting away from the outward (and inward) slavery that your abuser chained you into. It's all very profound... You are in danger of thinking that relationships are heavy, almost dangerous. However, making friends and falling in love, as important as those are to life, are things that happen naturally and freely, almost unconsciously. If a narcissist liked talking and receiving attention, that doesn't mean someone else's talking and getting attention has to be a sign of narcissism! You can allow yourself to give attention, and also to get the attention you merit in the situation.

If you start dating again in the right frame of mind, it could be a way to help you to break your trauma bond. We are not saying that this is the only, or the main reason, to go out with someone. The whole point is that people are ends in themselves, and not means to an end. Indeed, you mustn't use someone to help you to get what you want, for doing so is typically narcissistic; no, but you can date because it helps you to see how good life, and other people, can be. You are allowed to be hopeful for the future!

"What do I want out of dating?" If you aren't ready to think about the long-term, it's all right: don't criticize yourself. However, before the event, try to be clear about your expectations. Why not write some points for yourself, to help you to answer the question above? These points will not be about who you are looking for, but what you as a human being want to gain, and experience, from and by going out with someone. It's looking after yourself with a healthy self-love, the very thing you ignored when you became obsessed with a narcissist or traumatized person who took all your attention. It could help you in the unfortunate event that someone does turn out to be a 'Narc', or just too needy! You would see that you just weren't fulfilling any of your own goals for yourself by being in contact with them.

Do you want to be attracted to someone? Physically or emotionally? Would you like to find yourself imagining what a deeper link to them, a future with them, could be like? Would you like to feel life without obsessing about trauma?! You can take a break from looking after your soul. Would you enjoy the chance to express your warmth and affection, just for the sake of life?

Once these goals are clear enough, once you are honest enough to put them in writing (they don't have to be cut and dried yet!), then you can ask yourself what you are looking for in the person you will start dating. To have some happy moments is enough; moments are meaningful, no less than stories and sagas! A recovering victim is someone who is learning about love. To say, 'learning' is not to say, "getting head-knowledge of", because love is not a science, but an art. It has to be experienced and practised, to know it.

Returning to the question, "How will I know I'm ready for love?" it, too, doesn't have a studied answer. You may find that you stop asking, because you'll have just assumed that you are. (The same would apply in reverse, if you knew that you were still unready).

At this point we want to talk frankly about expectations in love. There are two extremes to be avoided: the sort of, "It's got to be perfect", and the "Any dream will do". Having a traumatic childhood, and, or, a traumatic adult relationship could push you into either one of them, depending on your personality and the experiences you had. Many statistics of perceived happiness in marriage have shown that a significantly higher percentage of women are unhappy with their relationships, compared to men. This is more certainly so in the Western world. Why? We suggest that there seems to be a tendency among men to expect too little, and among women, too much. Blame Hollywood? If you expect always to walk on air, or through beds of (thorn-less) roses, you'll hit disappointment! Turned around: if you decide that a bit of company, a bit of sex, and a little mutual help with organizing daily life, is all you need, you risk missing so many of the wonderful possibilities of another person, of a love-relationship! You risk giving too little, and therefore getting very little back.

Of course, for men and women, it can be the other way round, we don't deny. Finding Miss Perfect, however, is going to be a fearful, frustrating, unsuccessful task. Ditto Mr. Perfect... That's because she, and he, doesn't exist! When you have attained inner peace, and you've looked within yourself to care for yourself, then you will be able to accept someone else's faults more easily. You will be a lot less subjective, and won't have any fear of moving away from someone if you realize that their faults are too grave for you to be able to have a healthy relationship with them. You do have to tell yourself not to do what some parents do when they give "conditional love". Without loving someone's faults, you have to LOVE THEM AS THEY ARE, not for what you hope to make them, or they'll become.

It's true that many men find being alone after a relationship very difficult. It isn't just that men's sexual desire is less influenced by their moods (it certainly doesn't "switch off" when they are not in love, or hurting from disappointment in love), so that it continues to ache inside them; it is also true that their moods affect their daily routine of looking after themselves more, so that some feel almost unable to carry on eating, cleaning, organizing, and doing small daily tasks. Just don't rush into a new relationship out of desperation! The best things really are worth the wait. You need to face how you feel inside (including all that loneliness) and be logical about it. When you've spent time getting over your toxic 'ex', you'll be aware of how that 'Narc' affected you, and you will be more aware of yourself for the future, potentially in love, more aware as well of the kind of person you DON'T want in your life, and who you DO.

When you've been dating, now, for some time, and you've gone through these stages... what then? How will you know if you should let yourself fall in love? When will the time be to think about commitment? It will have to do with LESSENING OF FEAR, psychologists say. Letting time go by without rushing, and getting to know someone, the fear stirred up by your bad memories will grow less and less. It should do, at any rate, if all is well. It will seem better to grow closer, you'd sense more peace, than if you tried to pull away from your new acquaintance. You can always slow down the process; maybe you feel like speeding it up, only because it's good, NOT because you are afraid of losing someone!

Keep up the good habit of checking your emotions each day. Set some healthy boundaries of what you do and don't want, and accept the same from the one you are starting to love. How much time do you spend together? It doesn't have to be all your time. It's quite OK to be tired after a meal in a restaurant: you can say that you had a good date, but you need to go home to get ready for work the next day, and sleep. Would that be accepted? It should be: it's reasonable. That example is just exactly what marks a narcissistic personality. Those people want to control your time; they want to chat till one in the morning when they're in the mood (how can you be tired?). The next time, they'll finish the pudding in one gulp and say, "Well, I think it's time to go now." (As if you'd think otherwise!) The boundaries that are healthy for you are also boundaries inside YOU. For example, "I won't let myself be pushed into talking about my dysfunctional family members."

Keep moving forwards in your life: avoidance of intimacy is safe, and for a time after abuse, that makes sense. Yet a time comes when you need to live a fuller life. There is risk in dating: rejection, disappointment, and so on... but, take small risks; risk is a part of normal, healthy life. If a dating-relationship does fall down flat, think of this: compared to your past trauma bond, how much smaller it is! You can try again so much more easily. Don't be discouraged.

When will the trauma bond be out of the way in your relationships? Probably, you will start to 'thrive' almost without knowing. At first you counted good days where you weren't facing 'meltdown' of your emotions; later you lived a few days well, a day or so badly. When a time comes that you realize suddenly that a week has gone by without your thinking of your 'ex' or being reminded of them, then you can tell that their influence (that is, the trauma bond's influence) is becoming minimal. You are no longer controlled by it; rather, you are controlling your emotions, and your memory's in a healthy balance with your reason.

The first date might seem like a reunion of three: you, your new acquaintance, and the ghost of your 'ex' lurking around in the background. Ugh! Persevere: it will seem less and less like that, once your memories are being called to order and laid to rest. Eventually you'll be able to go out with someone and realize that you didn't think about your past abuser at all during that time, because the new person in your life just isn't that 'Narc' at all, nor anything to do with them. Don't worry if you find yourself 'trying' to be kind, sociable, attentive, etcetera, rather a lot at first. Making an effort isn't false or unhealthy! It should become second nature, with time. Trying to love, is actually loving.

Chapter 23
Trauma-Bonding Q & A, and Case-Studies

T he first part of this chapter takes the form of questions from fictional situations, that have been written to illustrate typical situations in which sufferers of trauma bonds can be found, and gives you some answers.

MUST I LEAVE MY PARTNER STRAIGHT AWAY?

My husband is a narcissist. He's a manipulator, I know it. We've been together for eight years and I feel emotionally empty and destroyed. I'm cut off from most of the family and friends I used to be in contact with, because nobody in the family has ever seen what he's like when he's mad at me, or how arrogant and uncaring he is when we're alone together. I ended up rowing with some of them because they just don't listen. Friends I had sometimes listened to me, but other times I felt some of them were just embarrassed to hear about my troubles. I also felt ashamed of myself, though now I'm learning why I shouldn't be. I left him once three years ago when I found out he'd had an affair. I went back after we talked things over, it was a sort of apology from him but quite honestly not much, and I had to promise never to mention it again. I don't know if he's done it again because he controls everything, and hides so much from me. I just went back to endless criticism and blazing rages from him. He doesn't hit me as such (does smash plates and furniture, etc. though) but he makes me so miserable. I know I should leave him, I intend to, but this is my problem. Two years ago we moved to the Middle East when he got a contract here. I'm like a prisoner. Not only does he hate it when I go out alone, the fact is I don't know anyone here. We don't have children. I'm totally financially dependent on him. When I read some of the advice about getting away from your abuser, it makes me feel bad, because right now I just don't think I can get on a plane and go. The thing is - his contract comes to an end in nine months. He doesn't want to stay here either, we talk about his plans to go back to our country where he wants to buy his dream house on a golf estate. I'm asking: can't I wait until we're back home? I really, really do know I should leave. What should I do?

ADVICE:

We have urged and almost pleaded abuse-victims to leave toxic relationships with someone who is not going to change by their staying. This is our basic advice, and counselors and therapists would say the same; BUT, we are aware that some victims are in dire straits, to use that expression. If you can learn how to handle a narcissist with indifference and calm, and you are not in physical danger, then perhaps you should wait, as you say. If you can get to a computer and find yourself a support-group, you will do well. You need to take control of your confused and scrambled thoughts, using reason to think clearly about your reactions, and to remind yourself of the truth. Stop trying to punish yourself, and realize that you can be caring to YOU, and look after your own well-being. Eat well and exercise at home, maybe! Just get ready for when you return, and plan ahead to find a way to make a decisive break then. You will need support after doing it, not just before. Your road to recovery has already started: it did when you saw your abuser for what he is. We wish you patience, and a firm will to do what is necessary: to take your life back!

DATING ADVICE NEEDED - IS THIS MAN A NARCISSIST?

I'm a widow who lost her husband three years ago. It was a happy marriage and I was devastated when my loving partner died. I had a difficult childhood when I felt unlovable because of having a damaged foot and leg, so that I've always walked with a limp. Recently I've met someone I saw a few times when shopping. One day he came up to me and introduced himself out of the blue. He said I looked really cute but really lonely. He offered to buy me a coffee. I felt flattered by his attention. He is an absolute film-star in looks for his age (we're in our sixties) and he said my limp makes no difference to him. He says he's divorced many years and comes to my city on business. I gave him my phone-number. He sent texts regularly and we met several times for a coffee. Then he messaged me to say he's fallen in love with me. I didn't know what to think! I let him take me out to the river for a boat-trip, and in the car arriving back, he kissed me and touched me rather appreciatively. Half of me felt really loved, but the other half feels guilty when I think of my husband dying only a short time ago. He also expects me to reply to all his texts, and gets impatient when I don't. He keeps on telling me about the beautiful house he has. I've told him that I like him, but that I don't know if I'm ready yet. I'm afraid he might go back to his city and I'll miss him, but I also wonder about him. If he's so good-looking, why is he still single after many years? Should I have let him take me in his car? Is he one of these 'Narcs' I'm reading about, 'love-bombing' me?

ADVICE:

You have every right to accept an invitation - to go out on a date. You can feel loved again, and open to the idea of just going for a coffee. Tell him you need time to get to know him: that's really a very reasonable request. Try to enjoy your conversations - if you feel you're being pushed, it's a sign that you are not at peace. With time, things should become clearer. Your childhood may have made you feel unlovable; remind yourself that it's not true! This may be behind your fear of losing him, and fear's not a good reason to stay in a friendship. If he becomes angry or disappointed with you, or just goes back to his city, it's a sign that things aren't right from his side of the equation, that he's not respecting you.

A FAMILY MEMBER WANTS TO RESCUE THE VICTIM

My sister has been married to an abusive husband for three years. My mother saw the bruises he inflicted on her stomach and hips, and my sister doesn't deny that he hits her and injures her physically. But she won't leave him! Sometimes she makes excuses for his behavior. After what I've read about trauma-bonding, I feel like driving to her house when her abuser isn't there, and telling her to pack a suitcase and get in, so that I could rescue her! What should I do?

ADVICE:

If your sister's injuries are severe, you should take her to a doctor; and if her life is in danger, contact the police at once. However, if her situation is somewhat less obviously dangerous, you could certainly try to persuade her to come with you.

The problem with a victim in a trauma-bond, if that is her situation, is the level of confusion that victim suffers, and the devastating feeling of loss and pain once the abuser is gone. She may panic and refuse to leave with you; or try to go back to her husband. You might decide to talk to her gently but firmly, and explain what a trauma bond is, and how it comes to be that part of her still wants to be with him, like an addict. Try to convince her that she needs help to be set free, such as a support-group and, or, a counselor; that she needs to work on herself, and that if she does, she will see clearly why she needed to leave that relationship.

CAN 'NARCS' BE MARRIED TO ONE ANOTHER?

I am working for a travel-agency that belongs to a married couple. I know he's a liar because we've all been put in embarrassing situations regarding our clients because of what he says and promises. We didn't get the perks we were promised by him. I don't deal with the books, but I know that things aren't right there. We three employees seem to fight one another instead of waking up and being united; we seem to be fed different information, and confused.

The wife appears to be confused as well, panicking and saying she finds running the business very hard. Yet it always happens that they owe her money, never the other way around; that if you tell him something, she doesn't know, and vice-versa. They're smart, well-spoken people who live a fast lifestyle, always away on trips to "check out" a luxury hotel, etc. Is she a 'Narc' as well? Wouldn't it be impossible for them to get on? Or is she suffering from the trauma bond?

ADVICE:

Does she really look as if she's enduring abuse? Trauma is exhausting and sickening to the body as well as the mind. If, as you say, she is as deeply involved as he is, and things always seem to work in her favor... Unfortunately, it is possible for narcissists to be a couple. They may despise one another... and they may still compete, yet together, in ways to crook and deceive others. Try to think clearly and don't let yourself be confused. Be patient with your fellow workers. Jobs are at a premium in today's world, so you may want to stay on. However, you may be better to find another job: the future of a dishonest business isn't very good, and you may become a victim, if you're not already.

CAN AN ABUSER WHO IS A NARCISSIST CHANGE AND BECOME A BETTER PERSON?

The first time my boyfriend hit me, I told my parents, and he was warned. He was very apologetic. The second time was months later, and I called the police. The same thing. We went on to have two children. He can be very funny and affectionate, and also withdrawn and depressed. However, he's as mean as a church mouse, and he's often away on gigs, because he's a musician. I can spend only what he allows me to, and the same for what I make from home. Sex is sex on demand... He's quite OK to talk to, even fascinating, but you can't disagree with him: if you do, you're wrong. He hit me a few times more over the course of our relationship, and recently I was hit again. I decided we needed relationship counseling, and we've been going for a while. He says he has a lot of anger-management problems from when he was a boy. I believe that, but I'm worried that he's actually a narcissist deep down. I look back on the five years we've known each other, and it seems I've had to change for him every time, never that he'd change or put himself out for me. Something about him is absolutely gorgeous in my eyes, but I wonder: with this counseling, can he actually change?

ADVICE:

If you've read the first chapters of this book: are you in a trauma-bond? It seems as if you are, and it's first things first, to heal yourself, so you can take control of where your life's heading. Then you can judge for yourself more clearly. Speak to the counselors, perhaps on your own, and ask them to help you (He can have his own sessions, as well). If your boyfriend really is a narcissist, then as far as you are concerned, he would NOT change, but be pathologically selfish to the end. In some circumstances a narcissist has to MODIFY his or her behavior, but that's just because it isn't possible to be so abusive or selfish for a time, for whatever reason. It's not a change of heart, and he or she will re-offend once the restriction is over. Read the case-studies and any other advice you can, to get an idea of what abusers are like. That could help you to decide what you should do about your relationship. What kind of a father is your boyfriend? What do other people think of him? We cannot judge here, but the most important thing for you is to respect yourself, accept that you've been trapped emotionally, and learn to grow as a person in the ways we have set out. It is not acceptable that he keeps hitting you.

FICTIONAL CASE-STUDIES TO ILLUSTRATE TRAUMA-BONDING AND TYPES OF ABUSE AND ABUSERS

COLLAPSED NARCISSISTS

We give two examples of these, and some explanation of their identifying schemes and characteristics. Firstly, the case of a female 'Collapsed Narcissist', "Bessie Bitterbrew"; and then a male of this kind, "Steven Syanight". Look through the details of the stories, and you will see what we've been talking about.

BESSIE BITTERBREW

Bessie Bitterbrew has been writing complaining, denouncing letters in the local newspaper for years. Her chief vendetta is against the hotel opposite her house. Every festive season there will be a complaint about the noise the guests are making; letters to the Town Council asking for more parking always refer snidely to the fact that there are cars belonging to hotel-guests parked along the road outside her house. The hotel manager has always tried to point out that the cars responsible are not those of hotel staff or guests. In any case, Bessie has very few visitors, and doesn't drive herself. Neighbors who had a genuine complaint against the hotel, namely that the giant oak tree at the side is growing over the roof of their house, so a falling branch could cause damage... wish they'd never mentioned it when they were at the Post Office. Bessie was there and heard them talking. A letter to the paper was published in which it said that they'd complained several times to the hotel, and were ignored (in fact, they'd mentioned it only once, to the gardener, and hadn't approached the hotel formally at that time, though they had meant to). The letter alleged that they were going to sue the hotel! Bad feeling all around resulted. The establishment was accused of being "seething with cockroaches" and causing a plague of the said insects in the area, though no-one else backed up her accusation. The manager had the Town Council spray all the rubbish-disposal area and wheeled bins, and had the kitchen fumigated by professionals, all at a cost of seven hundred pounds. He wrote to the paper to say so, to show potential guests and the neighbors that the Greenings Hotel was serious about public health. Bessie replied with a triumphant letter claiming that the fact of having the place sprayed was an admission of guilt!

Bessie tells every visitor she has, about the way she's been treated. Her son has nothing to do with her, never writes or calls; her sister is a "cow" who screamed at her the last time they met; her elder daughter is "an absolute angel" but she lives in Canada. The last time that daughter came, she took Bessie for a trip to Devon... but even though she's showed her the leaking roof in the bedroom, and her daughter promised to get someone to fix it for her, nothing's been done. She doesn't know what's going to happen to her health... damp, cold conditions... she bursts into tears.

In her younger days Bessie modeled fashion clothing. Her wealthy and long-suffering husband died quite a few years ago, and her money is running low, a fact that she readily admits. It would be no use to point out that she shops in high-class grocery-stores only, and uses a taxi rather than the 'bus most of the time. Her house is far too big for one person. Actually, it was a leak in one of the three spare bedrooms a year or so ago, but her nephew went up on the roof and fixed the tiles for her. She showed her daughter the marks on the ceiling, but Bessie hasn't had it put right, though she could afford to have it painted; or her nephew would probably fix that as well, if asked. Bessie's nephew was given a cup of tea for his efforts on the roof! The nephew is sent by her sister and brother-in-law as a sort of proof to the world that they are still family, but neither of them ever wants to see Bessie again, and Bessie's nephew is doing the work very reluctantly.

After her husband died, Bessie's youngest daughter came back to live with her, after much pleading. All three children grew up with her being a critical, complaining mother who expected them to do a lot of things for her, and who treated them like servants; though at times she would give them lavish praise when other people were present, or give them expensive gifts and make it known! All three have battled to do well in life: the elder daughter is divorced from an arrogant, abusive, compulsive liar who had many affairs. The younger daughter suffers from depression, though her mother rubbishes the idea, claiming that it's just an excuse for her not trying hard enough in life. After a few years of putting up with her mother, she went for some counseling, and thus the youngest daughter saw through her mother: Bessie Bitterbrew is a narcissist! This daughter ended up meeting and falling in love with a local man, and they decided to marry and go to live in London. Bessie, who'd never liked the boyfriend, threw a tantrum when told they wanted to get married, and then shortly after, on knowing that her daughter was leaving, flew into a rage of screaming and crying. "You selfish parasite! I looked after you, and you pay me back by leaving me all alone!!" Unfortunately, her daughter replied in kind, with shouting and tears. Bessie's younger daughter offered to pay for help at home for her mother, which was accepted begrudgingly.

Bessie wasn't at her youngest's wedding. The daughter didn't want her mother to be there, but the brother and sister, who also didn't really want her there, persuaded her to send an invitation all the same. The invitation was destroyed, and Bessie never answered any 'phone calls from them. That's what they'll tell you. Yet if you see Bessie at the Post Office, you'll hear her complaining about "my runaway daughter" who married a "dodgy-looking mechanic's son" and pushed off to London, "...and never even invited me to her wedding!"

Yes, Bessie Bitterbrew is a narcissist, collapsing as her health fails, and fewer and fewer people want to know her. Yes, it's true that her son hardly ever contacts her, and that her sister shouted at her the last time they met: when you know how Bessie behaved to them over the years, you understand why! Her son spent years listening to and suffering from her acid criticisms: she never thanked him for anything he ever did for her, no matter how much, till he'd had enough. His father had just stayed silent all along. As for the sister: Bessie spread false rumors that her brother-in-law was having an affair... (she was really just jealous that her sister still had a husband, whereas she'd lost hers). As she grows ever more hateful and bitter, Bessie accuses the hotel manager publicly of having prostitutes working there, and, he having gone through a divorce, of being a client himself. She accuses the husband-neighbor next to the oak tree (now trimmed back). Someone hit the corner of his car when he was driving at night; he's known for being rather jolly at parties. So she accuses him anonymously in the letters to the Editor of the newspaper, of being a drunken driver whose license ought to be confiscated!

So, how does this illustrative story end? When her health is too bad, and there's no money left to look after the house - for real - the children find Bessie a place in the Retirement Home. After refusing to go for months, they have to confront her and take her there. She screams so much and cries so loudly that the whole suburb hears: "You merciless, money-grabbing thieves! Help me! They're taking away my home! They're throwing me in the 'loony bin'!! It's a prison in there!" She has to be tranquilized. For a year and a half Bessie is the black sheep of the Retirement Home. She complains about every member of staff. The food is never right. The others are all "ga-ga", i.e. mad... This is where Bessie gets her nickname-surname: "Bitterbrew". The male nurse, apparently, made advances on her. The few visits she has from her family all end up in her arguing and shouting, pleading to be allowed to go to a better place. She weeps, and says that people there are trying to label her as "the black sheep of her family" when all she ever wanted was the best for them. Her health has actually improved, since she is (despite what she says) eating well and more healthily. She cries for hours on end, telling the staff what they've heard so many times - that she's been deserted. The day before her elder daughter arrives from Canada to see her mother (separately) and siblings, Bessie gets the new, young care-assistant to walk with her to the Pharmacy/Chemist, which he's not supposed to do. She buys non-prescription pain-killers. In the Retirement Home, she is allowed to manage her own medicines. Bessie's been taking sleeping-tablets for some years. That night, she takes all the pain-killers and all the sleeping-tablets she had for that week. When she doesn't appear for breakfast, a carer goes to her room, to find her dead from the overdose. There is a suicide-note. It reads, "YOU THREE LEAVE ME NO CHOICE. SIGNED, YOUR MOTHER."

What can we see in this story? Bessie was obviously a narcissist who used her rich but passive husband, lived an elegant lifestyle, and regarded her children as suitable servants whom she could recruit for her play called "loving mother" which she put on occasionally. Her feelings of superiority and entitlement may not have produced the worst abuse, but she affected her children severely, aided by the passivity of their father. However, once her 'narcissistic supply' decreased (her husband's death, her son's distancing himself, and her eldest's moving to Canada), her world began to shrink. Her bitter letters reveal a dissatisfaction with the world for not being as she wanted it, and their gossiping tactics show a mind that had the power to inflict destruction and conflict among her neighbors. Her soliciting sympathy follows a trajectory: recruiting new people and telling a believable story to elicit a loving response; crying and begging, and finally childlike tears and tantrums. To the end, she saw people to use, and was successful in using them. Her final decision to die was timed as a vindictive revenge on the only child who still visited her, and a swipe out to include the other two, to make them all feel shame, which is what her lifelong criticism had done to them already.

All of Bessie's children, and her sister, followed a type of No-Contact policy with her. We may be able to see, as her daughter might have afterwards, that shouting and losing one's temper has little effect on a narcissist - other than to encourage them to take revenge. The youngest daughter was being damaged by her mother even as she was supposed to be helping her, when she moved back. By no means are we saying, and we do not mean, that someone is wrong to move back to help an elderly parent. What we describe is a 'Narc' who has absolutely no respect or gratitude, and who treats this self-sacrifice as nothing. However, Bessie's younger daughter came to see that she was a victim, and acted in an assertive way. We can only hope that she has learned not to be a victim, nor to be a narcissist, herself! To sum up this tragedy: Bessie damaged not only a family of three children, traumatizing especially the one who, ironically, was the closest at the end (who formed a trauma-bond with a man whose harsh nature seemed like a remedy to her father's passivity)... but an entire network of people. The neighbors angry with the hotel and the hotel with them; money wasted on fumigation; her sister and brother-in-law insulted and their son working for nothing; the staff of the Retirement home, where a room was left empty during the months Bessie refused to go, then they were made to waste time and money trying to look after her because she demanded so much attention; then the young assistant got into trouble, and the nurses in trouble for not administering all the residents' medicines personally, making sure if every one is taken, and when... The true cost of one abuser is more than it appears, and it is staggering!

STEVEN SYANIGHT

On birthdays and in the festive season one finds glittering parties at the house of Steven Syanight. He was a successful businessman, and now he's semi-retired. He and his wife are the perfect hosts: well-educated, smartly-dressed, urbane and able to talk pleasantly to all those whom they invite. Steven can be the master of ceremonies with ease; he can remember something interesting about each guest, so when he introduces you to someone you haven't met before, he can tell you that the new guest works in plant-breeding, and that "Ivan has a variety of kiwifruit named after him!" They have a beautiful house with a verdant palm-fringed garden, and their adult children live nearby.

What you won't know is that once the last guest is gone, Steven is a tyrant. He barks orders at his wife, who we begin to see is tired and haggard. She enjoys the parties because they are some of her few opportunities to be happy, meet the family and other people - and the only times Steven is a pleasure to be with. Steven goes to his beloved bar and entertainment area, where he does clean and tidy it. However, ninety percent of the tidying-up is in the rest of the house. When Steven's finished his part and poured himself another drink, his wife, their daughter and son-in-law are washing dishes, finding glasses, and mopping the floor in the rest of the house. The son-in-law avoids Steven. Soon their daughter and son-in-law are driving away: the son-in-law hates the way Steven treats his wife and her mother, and just wants to leave. The daughter feels sorry for her mother - she knows exactly what it is like to live in the same house as Steven, and to endure his endless mockery and outbursts of anger. When Steven comes into the kitchen and throws something in the trash-can, he sees a broken glass. He flies into a rage: "WHO THREW THIS IN HERE?" he demands to know. His face is an inch from Rebecca's face (his wife's): "Are you gonna tell me you didn't remember this is Waterford Crystal?!" He storms out, slamming the door behind him so hard that the next-door neighbors hear. That was an average rage: if pushed to tell, by their son, Rebecca would admit that slapping her on the face, or pushing her to the floor, would be a "bad " rage. Their son and his wife left the party immediately that it ended. They know exactly what he's like. Rebecca's son has had arguments with his mother, because she just puts up with him. He cannot understand why.

Steven Syanight drinks every day. It would be rare to see him drunk, however: he has too much pride and self-respect to be like that. He is also incredibly mean. Every time his best car is sent to the mechanic, he will dispute what they did, call the work "backyard quality" and try to lower the bill. He's lost his temper so badly, recently, that they threatened to call in the police if he didn't calm down. The active businessman Steven was a hard bargainer, but knew when to stop. However, after semi-retiring, there isn't enough to occupy him, and he is becoming bitter, bored and frustrated. His work as a member of the board of directors seems to be turning into nothing more than occasional stirring-up of conflicts. He's a clever man, but his knowledge wasn't always used generously, and he was more feared than liked, by his subordinates.

Steven and Rebecca have a large tropical garden which is the envy of the island. It requires a lot of maintenance, and there are two gardeners. The older man has been there for years. He just sighs and says that he has to be thankful for his job, and the chance to work in a tropical climate that he'd never have had if he'd stayed in Wyoming. The other one keeps changing, because they walk off the job one by one. Nothing is good enough for Steven. Not only is he impossible to satisfy, but he pays far too little.

The business community, Steven's only real "friends", know little about these abuses and problems, though some of them have heard rumors. Their neighbors know, but say nothing. The palm-trees and greenery hide the magnificent house, but don't stop the sound.

In his increasing spare time, Steven is a member of the committee of the Orchid Society. When a couple of members had an outbreak of pests in their collections, Steven's pushing-through of the motion banning them from plant-shows for a whole year, and ordering them to give a detailed description of their pesticide-treatments, was held to be unnecessarily harsh. He had some stand-up arguments with members. Another odd, significant thing one junior member recalls, is the case of the Cryptolatrium. This rare orchid was grown successfully by him, and Steven was one of the few who were invited to visit when it was flowering. It'd had four new buds on the base, and the next day this member found that there were only three. If it had fallen off, where was the detached bud? He never found it. A year or two later, a friend of the junior member had a tour of Steven's gorgeous orchid collection. He happened to see a young specimen in the nursery-area, and its unusual leaves called his attention. On coming home, the friend looked up Cryptolatrium online, and confirmed that it was one. He told his friend, but they feared Steven's temper too much to make a complaint, and there was another reason they kept quiet: the junior member didn't have a license to grow this endangered species. Steven had the knowledge to grow something as difficult as Cryptolatrium from a bud, though it was obvious that affording a mature specimen was quite within his means. Steven actually spent money, and so managed to get a license to grow Cryptolatrium...

Steven's son and daughter-in-law grew to hate living near him, because the father's effect on his son was so negative. Steven had an endless list of insults for his son: "Retard", "blockhead", "layabout" and "good-for-nothing" being the most printable. Steven's daughter-in-law came from an Italian-American family and hated his endless jokes and remarks about them: "Why didn't you kiss me on both cheeks? Aren't you people supposed to be touchy-feely?" She battled to lose weight: "Well, we can all see YOU lika da pasta, hey?" They had two children, whom Steven certainly seemed to love, and was very affectionate towards. However, he used to take them for rides in the back of his pick-up truck, driving down to the beach at breakneck speed. The little girls loved it, but their parents were horrified. Steven's daughter-in-law stated very firmly: "Dad, unless you have them in the cab with you, and seat-belts on, they're NOT going for a ride with you, ever again. We cannot risk their lives. Do you really want to be responsible for the death or injury of your grandchildren?" His son stood up to him for a change and said, without shouting, that he was in full agreement. When Richard protested that they were trying to use the grandchildren to settle their disagreements with him, his son said simply, "Oh, come on, Dad. We're keeping them safe. Period." Steven gave in, but he was sullen and complaining for the next week or so.

Several things went wrong for Steven in the next few years. Firstly, his son and daughter-in-law sold their house without telling the parents, and then announced they were moving to Seattle. He flew into a rage and accused them of trying to cut him off from his grandchildren, and Rebecca burst into tears, but they went ahead and moved. Steven changed his will without telling them, leaving them out of his estate.

Then disaster struck Rebecca, and she suffered a serious stroke. After some time in hospital, and some months having a maid at home (Rebecca had never been allowed to have help in the home before), she was able to walk, but had to use a stick, and slurred her words. The foreign maid left rather quickly, Steven insulting her memory afterwards in the hearing of other people: "That stupid little slit-eyed girl didn't know the difference between a vacuum-cleaner and a floor-polisher!" Just before she left, the maid told Rebecca that he tried to grope her. Steven's wife, unusually for her, confronted him about it. Unusually for him, he didn't lose his temper. He just replied coldly: "So what if I did? Am I supposed to be satisfied sleeping with a spastic like you?"

Rebecca told her daughter. She looked miserable and worn-out. Her daughter, frustrated by her mother, but also sorry for her, asked, "Do you still love Dad? After all this?" Rebecca just replied, "I... don't know." Rebecca needed handles in the bathroom and on the stairs in what was a split-level house. No handles were ever fitted. "This house was designed by the best architect in Honolulu. Do you wanna make it look like a ******* hospital? Get a maid if you need one!" The last was said with vicious, deep sarcasm.

Stephen started drinking more and working less. He attended the Orchid Society hardly at all. His daughter, now a mother of twins, came less and less often to see her parents. Finally, one evening, he went out in the pickup truck, in a bad mood, to get some groceries because Rebecca could no longer drive. He'd been drinking, and the vehicle left the road and rolled. Steven was taken to hospital with multiple injuries. He was the world's worst patient: he shouted so much that they ended up knocking him out with sedatives. After leaving hospital, his daughter and son-in-law arranged for home nursing, since Rebecca couldn't help much.

Steven decided, in an instant, that everything was too much to look after, and he sold their house, most belongings, and car. The right decision, probably, but he did it with shouting and crying, leaving Rebecca and their children out of any of the arrangements. He and Rebecca moved to a retirement village where they had a beautiful cottage, home nursing, and endless arguments wherein he shouted, and she cried helplessly. Their few visitors heard him complaining about their lazy, spendthrift son, and raging and crying about his daughter-in-law, whom he called a prostitute, who "stole their grandchildren and took them away from us". His daughter came a few times, but without his youngest grandchildren. He would ask why, and she had replied that he was too drunk and too upsetting for them to see! This sent him into floods of tears, and more volleys of shouting: "You don't love me any more, do you? What am I supposed to have done?"

Steven had his own stroke after two years. So now he sits silently in the wheelchair. He has mellowed: he cannot speak, though he can signal with one hand. Sometimes his eyes fill with tears when he sees his youngest grandchildren, old enough now to understand who Grandpa is, and why he cannot talk. At other times he stares emptily. Rebecca is frail, but more at peace. She says, "I suppose the worst is over. I think I can feel sorry for him now."

This story, dear recovering victim, is about one victim above all the many others... Rebecca. Rebecca sacrificed most of her life and happiness, because she wouldn't see that she was just there to be used by a pathologically-selfish Steven. Was his charming 'act' at parties the mirage that led her to marry him? Were these the moments she tried to cling to? Someone like Rebecca illustrates the wicked waste of life when a victim cannot see what is happening. Her son and daughter did not understand trauma-bonding, and perhaps their challenging their mother could have been gentler but even firmer, if they had. However, in the case of joyriding with his grandchildren, the way to be very firm but calm has been illustrated, and the daughter-in-law turns the responsibility to Steven: if he loves them, then...?This caused what psychology would call a "modification of behavior" in Steven. This is not a change of heart, though it is, if it can be enforced, a way to manage a narcissistic personality. Perhaps Steven's son, in Seattle now, will fly into a rage every now and then. His wife will call him out on it, and say that she's afraid he may turn out to be like his Dad. Hopefully, shocked and ashamed, he will seek counseling, and find that he is wounded by his Dad's lovelessness and bad example in childhood. It's not his fault - what happened in his past - yet he can and must change his behavior in the present, for the sake of their future. The odd little incident of the Cryptolatrium orchid is a case of the narcissistic entitlement driving a wealthy man to steal from someone he considered unworthy of having a privilege. It's very diagnostic of a certain type of sociopath. As with Bessie, Steven injured, cheated, robbed (even emotionally), wasted and disturbed hundreds of people in his life. If we were to sum up the total cost of his damage, would it not run into millions? The personal unhappiness he caused cannot be put into figures - and it is greater still. Someone ought to calculate the economic and social damage one such individual can do! Yet consider this: if you can be set free from a trauma bond with help, and your own inner commitment, the rewards go beyond what money can buy.

TRAUMA BONDS IN A FAMILY: PARENT BONDED TO CHILD

It is not always that children become traumatically-bonded to a parent, or a lover to the beloved; it can happen that a devoted parent is the victim. There is a certain type of narcissist who is the perpetual beggar. The amount that one of these abusers can get out of people may be staggering, though they inevitably come to grief, as do those who don't break their bonds with them.

PADDY SPONGETAKE

They moved into the rented flat one day: a mother in her sixties, her son Paddy, and his girlfriend. No-one knew them. The first contact was when Paddy Spongetake knocked on the door of Anne, a neighbor. Paddy seemed well-dressed and well-spoken. He explained calmly, but without looking up, that they'd just moved from Sydney, and he was going to start working in the Grand Hotel the next month. However, their money was running out in the meantime, because they had just his Mum's pension to live on, and that wasn't coming till the end of the month. Could Anne (he'd asked her name) help them?

Anne's mind felt a bit of confusion, but she was a kind woman, and she said, "Just wait there." She closed her door, went to her handbag and found twenty dollars. She opened the front door again, and gave it to

174

Paddy. He looked grateful. He said, "Thanks. Sorry - could I ask you something?"

"OK," said Anne cautiously. She was a bit suspicious.

"You see, my girlfriend's still looking for work. If you happen to know anyone who needs a childminder, or maybe an old person who needs help with housework, or a restaurant needs a waitress - please let me know. We're staying at number thirteen."

"Of course I will," said Anne (somewhat relieved it wasn't another request for her to do something directly), "I can't think of anyone right now, but if I do, I'll let you know."

Anne was a widow who was active in charity organizations, her local church, and her bridge club. She still grieved for her husband, but she kept herself busy, and she liked living in a small town by the sea, where people knew one another. The next day, she had an idea, and when she went downstairs she stopped at number 13, and hung a bag on the doorknob. In it she'd put a few cans of food, and three oranges (for Vitamin C!).

Occasionally Anne would see Paddy coming and going from the flats when she was on her balcony; more rarely, his mother Linda and girlfriend Carla. Linda was thin and quiet, and Carla even thinner ("Anorexic?" wondered Anne) with dark circles around her eyes and pale, unhealthy skin. Anne got an opportunity to speak to Linda one day, and introduced herself.

Linda talked quietly but quite readily. It seemed that she had been quite sick for a couple of years, and then Paddy lost his job. Carla had already stopped working in order to help her Mum-in-law, so it was a disaster. They were really fed up with city life, and when the job offer for Paddy came along, they were happy to move. Linda said that her house in Sydney was for sale, but that economic conditions being as bad as they were, there was little interest from potential buyers. She thought of renting it, but Paddy, who handled all these things, was against the idea: where were they going to live in the meantime, and for how much?

Anne tried to be as sympathetic as she could. She said to Linda: "By the way, here in this town we have a Soup-Kitchen. Actually, we call it "M.T.'s Meals" after the initials of the founder. They give out on Monday and Thursday currently. Please don't feel ashamed to go; you can mention my name."

The next day, Wednesday, Anne went to the soup-kitchen premises to tell them about Linda. They said, "Don't worry, someone was here last week, and we've got her name down."
"Last week?" said Anne. "That's a bit quick, isn't it?" she thought.
"Yes, I think it was her son," said someone. "He said you knew them."

At the Grand Hotel, Paddy did a rather casual job in the kitchen. He knew how to make the food - of that there was no doubt - but he tended to let other people finish his work for him, to go off and take "smoke-breaks", usually going to the toilet for a long time. Some of the staff said they could smell drink when he talked, especially after his lunch-break. After three weeks on the job, one day he didn't turn up for work. He called later in the day to explain that he'd gone down with a cold, but sounded very casual about it. He returned the next day, calm and una-pologetic, looking somewhat sick, but not the way you look when you have a cold.

The Grand Hotel was known for its famous Christmas pudding: a real traditional fruit-cake type, bitter and rich. To adapt it to the reality of the Australian summer, it was served in the hotel restaurant with ice-cream and brandy-butter. It was highly popular, and because it needed to mature, it was made in September every year. Quite a lot of brandy went into the pudding, not to mention the brandy-butter. Strangely enough, that year a whole lot of brandy seemed to be needed for the Christmas pudding. Paddy had been given the recipe, and the staff were so familiar with it, anyway... so why had it needed three bottles more than the year before?

This discrepancy, and the fact that Paddy was absent for another two days with no doctor's note and no explanation other than calling in on the second day to say that his mother and his girlfriend were sick with the 'flu, meant that when he returned, it being the end of the month, he was given a warning. A couple of days later, being told quietly by one of the staff, the hotel manager looked in Paddy's bags and found a half-full bottle of brandy there. Paddy had the flimsiest of explanations, and was fired, being paid for the month, and to be fair to him, for one week of the next.

Somehow the family carried on. Not everyone knew that Paddy had been dismissed. Another neighbor, who knew Anne, got a request from Paddy one day. Paddy asked if he could borrow his car. He'd pay him for the petrol; he had to take his girlfriend Carla to the hospital, which was in the next town, for a check-up. Brian, the neighbor, was willing to help, but wanted to suggest that Carla's appointment be on a Friday, which was the next day, because he was going to town then. Paddy said calmly, but very quickly, that the appointment was already made, and it would have to be on the Monday. So Brian let him have the car.

A few days later, having returned the car to Brian (paying him ten dollars, which was probably half the value of the petrol used), Paddy turned up with another request: could Brian come to look at the cooker in the house? Brian was beginning to wonder about Paddy and his family, but agreed, and came to find that all three of the family were at home. Glasses of wine were perched on tables: Paddy said casually, "Sorry about the drink. It's my birthday today." Brian began to wonder if Paddy had a birthday several times a week, maybe every day...

"I'm not a certified electrician," cautioned Brian, but he ended up fixing the stove, since it was quite straightforward. The next day, he heard that Paddy had been fired from the Grand Hotel for stealing alcohol, and absenteeism. The family wasn't seen much of for a time.

A few months later, Linda knocked on Anne's door. Anne welcomed her in, but you could see that Linda was looking ill and tired. Linda explained that they were in terrible trouble. She asked if Anne knew about Paddy's looking for work because he'd lost his job at the Grand Hotel. She did. She said that Carla, Paddy's girlfriend, was very ill, and that she didn't know what they could do, because they couldn't pay the rent for their flat. They hardly had enough to eat. Anne asked Linda if Paddy was still drinking. Linda looked shameful, and replied that he was. So then Anne asked Linda if there wasn't a way for her to find her own accommodation, because clearly her son was drinking her pension money!

Linda cried. She explained that she had no control over her pension or finances. Anne pleaded with her: could she not draw the money herself using her bank card? She replied that her son had it. Could she not get hold of it? No, said Linda. She couldn't do that to her son. He'd be so upset with her. Could Anne not give them a bit of extra food?

Anne found herself before a slave, as she began to see Linda. Paddy was the one in charge, and Linda, and Carla, were dragged along with him. She steeled herself and said, "Linda, I'm sorry. I want to help you. I know of someone who's prepared to have you to stay with them, but it's only on condition that it's you alone, and that you have your identity card and bank card, which I'm going to keep for you. Paddy and Carla, we can have going to the soup kitchen. Unless you help yourselves, we can't help you." Linda looked worn out. She just got up, and without saying more, she went to the door, and walked out.

Brian saw Paddy walking down the road, later. He greeted Paddy, but had only this for a reply: "A bunch of ******* skinflints you are in this town! My girlfriend's dying, and you people don't want to help us!" This angered Brian, and he countered, "Young man, we've all done things to help you. You've been going to M.T.'s Meals for months. You have an offer to look after your mother for you, and I let you use my car to take Carla to the District Hospital, even though I could have taken her the next day. Right now, if she needs to stay in hospital, I'll take her - right now! But until you admit that you've got a drinking problem, I don't think we can help you any more. Do you want me to take Carla to hospital?" Paddy just turned round and walked away.

Linda never came to anyone with her bank card and identity documents. A week or two later, the three of them, Paddy, Linda and Carla (the latter looking like a concentration-camp victim), were seen getting into a van with some suitcases, and a driver took them away. Where to? Who are the next victims? And what will happen to Carla and Linda? Or Paddy, for that matter?

This is the tragic case of a mother who was so devoted to, and blinded by, her son that she let him take over her life. He's ruining them all, and we can understand why she became helpless in trauma-bonding, even doing some of her son's begging for him. He's a slave to alcohol. Carla, too, is bonded in trauma to her boyfriend, and a slave to alcohol as well. None of them is eating properly, not even Paddy, but he has managed to eat something. Linda probably goes without, that the others eat. Carla is sick, but Paddy won't have her to stay in hospital unless it's on his terms, which is probably that you gave them money.

Unless one could convince Linda, and Carla, that Paddy is heading for destruction and taking them all with them, there is little one can do. Linda is aware that things are bad, but she feels that she can't leave them, even though it would be the most loving thing to do, if you think about it.

We will always have the poor with us, and charity will always be needed. Yet we must ask how much of social welfare and charitable donations is wasted by people like Paddy, a 'Narc' with a feeling that the world must give him a living, and that his drinking is under control as long as they have a roof over their heads, and who feels sorry for no-one except himself.

THE LOVE-'EM-AND-LEAVE-'EM SOCIOPATH: PROMISCUOUS AND ABUSIVE, BUT THEY HAVE DEVOTED VICTIMS

The male 'Narcs' of this type are too commonly known to need much more explanation, but their female counterparts can be horribly successful in victimizing their prey over a long period of time, and in influencing, actually abusing their children out of a primal jealousy. We give the story of an exemplary female parasitical, promiscuous type.

179

SONIA SUMMERWYNE

When Réne first saw Sonia Summerwyne, her pale green eyes made an impression on him that wouldn't go away. Her manner was so fascinating, and she chatted to him in a lively way. After meeting her at the café several times, Réne knew he was falling in love. He could remember saying to her, "I think you're making an impression on me!" The next week, Sonia wasn't there! Halfway through the week after, she turned up again: "Oh, hi! I was just on holiday to see my uncle and his family." Réne realized that he'd missed her terribly.

He frequented the café more and more after work, and sought out Sonia. They talked more and more, and he was overjoyed that she listened to him so eagerly. He told her all about his life and dreams. Réne had had a hard childhood, missing his French-speaking father who died when he was seven, and always struggling to meet his mother's expectations that he'd be the kind of journalist his Dad had been. He loved his mother, now very old (and saw quite a lot of her), who had money to get things done, but at times she wanted Réne to do them instead, taking a bit too much of his time and attention.

Sonia spoke a bit about her family, but not much. She did make clear that apart from the uncle and his children, she wasn't close to them. She said she could understand what it was like to have an unhappy childhood. Usually, she moved onto the subject of Réne and his work: "Tell me, you've been to Kuwait? You covered the Gulf War? How amazing!"

Réne made love to her a couple of weeks after. He felt so loved that it was as if he were floating on air; love had never felt like that in his life before! He did feel, on waking up with her in his arms, that he might have been going a bit too fast... Nevertheless, he proposed to her a month afterwards, Sonia accepted with joy, and they planned a tropical honeymoon vacation in Mauritius; which sounded really exotic to Sonia, and which Réne knew, his father having been born there.

Quite a lot of the money for the honeymoon came from Réne's mother, who was quite taken with Sonia, although she wondered quite openly if her only son was going to have enough time to see her three times a week, as he had been doing when he was not reporting abroad, which he seldom did in those days. He bought things for her, fixed things in her home, and listened to all her stories, or her aches and pains! His sister was a more independent character who tended to restrict their mother's demands; she lived several hundred kilometers away, in any case.

Réne's and Sonia's first child was born within a year of their marriage. About a month after the wedding, Sonia complained that her car, which she'd had before, wasn't good enough, and was costing too much to repair. Réne was a bit worried about how he was going to buy the model she suggested, but he borrowed money without telling anyone, and got a cheaper car, but still brand new. Sonia was disappointed that it wasn't what she'd suggested: it was as if Réne'd thrown a bucket of cold water in her face. That was the first incident. Réne protested that he didn't earn that much; Sonia countered that he should have got his mother to help him!

When the baby was born, no gift was too much. Little Wendy's baby shower was more of a cloudburst of presents. Of course, Sonia had maternity leave and pay, but her husband saw that she was spending it lavishly. On their visits to show his Mom the new baby, Réne's mother found Sonia rude, and very possessive of the little one.

Another year went by, and Sonia was expecting her second child. Réne noticed that Sonia went in cycles: she could be the jade-eyed, flirtatious, sociable woman he'd met, and after a week or two, go into a bad mood where she barked orders at him, became irritatingly withdrawn, and didn't want sex. He wondered if she suffered from bipolar depression, but when she was in a bad mood she could snap out of it remarkably quickly when someone else was there. It made him feel guilty; deep down, Réne was always wondering if he was good enough. His escapades in foreign countries had been egged on by a desire to be successful, respectable, able to be taken seriously.

Réne was still thrilled when Barbara was born. He loved being a father, and it made up for the fact that Sonia seemed to be disappointed in him. One day he asked her out in the open, if something was wrong with him. She replied: "You don't let me love my children. I feel as if I'm competing with you!" Tears rolled down from her green eyes. Réne was absolutely surprised by what she said: he could never have guessed. He tried to explain, but Sonia just seemed to say "I've said what I've said, it's over now." Yet it wasn't. Réne took Sonia out for a few good meals in a restaurant, and got a babysitter, just so they could be together a bit.

When they visited Réne's sister and her husband and family, Sonia could be downright rude. After an hour and a half, to the second, she looked at Réne and snapped, "Come on, Ré! We have to get back. The kids are tired." Réne's sister Valerie really disliked Sonia, but for the sake of her brother, she suppressed it. The bad manners!

Barbara was quite small when Sonia went back to work. Sonia didn't rush back home each day; she seemed to have time to have a coffee with friends. Sonia also had a lot of time for HER family, being the uncle she was close to and his children. Visits to them were never cut short; she could demand to see them with almost no forewarning. Réne was expected to change his plans on the spot. Usually, he did. Sonia hated her aunt, the uncle's wife, though why that was so was not clear.

Five years into his marriage, Réne was deeply disappointed by it all. Sonia was so critical of him. Nothing he did, including a family holiday with the little ones in Mauritius again (thanks to his mother's help!) was ever good enough. He did love his daughters, though! Even in this, he started to feel that Sonia was the one who didn't let him love them as he wanted to. Then, some unpleasant rumors reached his ears: Sonia was said to be seeing someone for coffee at a local restaurant, quite often. He felt frozen with fear. He decided to say nothing, because as hard as it was to live with her, he dreaded losing the closeness of his children, and he kept on seeing the cool, fascinating light in Sonia's eyes as it had been when he'd first met her...

Réne's mother died soon afterwards. Sonia wasn't at all helpful with all the arrangements, though Valerie was. It was about this time that the rumors about Sonia's "new flame" she was seeing at the restaurant became too frequent, and Réne went there one day in the afternoon. There was Sonia outside at a table, kissing and making out with a big, dangerous looking guy. He confronted her: "Sonia! What the hell are you doing?"

"I think you have eyes, sweetie." She turned round, back to her beau.

There was quite an argument at home, but as angry as Réne was, he was feeling hopeless. Sonia burst into tears and said that she just felt she was kept at home like a pet, and for the sake of her children, that she felt Réne didn't love her any more. Réne could have said that was what HE felt like... Sonia went away to stay with her uncle, taking the children. On his own, Réne started drinking.

Yet Sonia came back, almost theatrically! She cried and said that she was sorry; but she pleaded with Réne to go with her for marriage-counseling. He agreed, and it seemed to work. Sonia opened up all about how unhappy her parents' marriage had been, and how insecure she felt as a mother; all with many tears. Réne did a bit of opening up, as well. They seemed to be loving again, and things ended up with their going away together (children looked after by her uncle and nephews) for a "second honeymoon", and Réne giving Sonia another diamond ring! All this was possible with what Réne had inherited from his mother, by the way.

The "honeymoon period" lasted a year and a bit, and Sonia seemed to become cold and unresponsive again for no apparent reason. Réne tried everything, but it just didn't work. The blow came when she told him out of the blue that she wanted a divorce. "You're a sad old drunkard!" she snarled. By this time, he was too exhausted to fight it.

Sonia went, demanded and got, a good settlement from her first husband. Hardly two months later, he heard that she was engaged to her manager at work! Soon after he was told that she was pregnant! It seemed that she'd been having an affair, well-hidden this time. The child was born, and he wasn't Réne's. On his own, instead of being free, Réne grieved for the first years of their marriage. He lived for the times he saw Wendy and Sonia, but there were endless arguments about his seeing them. She called him a useless father and an alcoholic. The second part was becoming true...

Valerie recalled going with Réne once, to see his children. She still remembers the look of concentrated hate they fixed her with. How could these happy little children change so much? They softened during their visit, but looked sad and confused. A year later, and the girls were with Valerie and her child, until Réne should come home from work. She asked about their Christmas. Wendy seemed upset. She muttered, "We got the magic unicorns we wanted, from Daddy. But Mommy was angry with him and she told us to bring them to the lounge. She put them on the fire and burnt them. She says he doesn't love us."

Valerie was horrified. Wendy was missing her Dad, but Barbara didn't seem so sure. Réne was told about it, and broke down. He said that he wanted to plead with Sonia to come back to him; that he would stop drinking if she did; anything to make Wendy and Barbara happy. That made Valerie exasperated: she asked Réne how he could have put up with a selfish parasite like Sonia for so long; couldn't he try to get custody of their children? Yet Réne just sighed, for he knew how hard that would be. Valerie asked, "But you don't still love Sonia, do you?"
"I don't know what to say. But anything's better than what I have now."
"But she's EVIL! Can't you see that?!"

Valerie, too, felt helpless. She talked to friends about what she saw happening to her nieces, and how Sonia had behaved. Sonia had received half of everything Rene had, which was a good part of the inheritance Réne and Valerie had received from their late mother. Someone mentioned "narcissistic entitlement", and Valerie stumbled on a world of explanation for Sonia and her treatment, that Réne had endured so passively. Réne was in a trauma bond with Sonia, and Sonia was in it for all she could get, especially Réne's money (presumably, her former boss and new husband's as well...)!!

184

She realized that her approach to helping her brother had been too angry and too challenging, and decided to explain what she had seen happening to him, gently but firmly. Réne wasn't happy about the idea of going to counseling, seeing that Sonia had managed to rig the last lot he'd attended, in her favor, not Réne's! In the end, he went to see a psychologist who had been recommended to his sister. With this man's help, he began to understand how his need for love and acceptance had been played with and hijacked, and what sort of a person Sonia, née Summerwyne, was. He started to work on his repeating thoughts of helplessness and inadequacy, and also his flashbacks to their honeymoon(s) in Mauritius, which he treated as if they were as horrifying as a war veteran's... because they were, being so false and so deceiving!

Handling Sonia calmly but without any sign of upset or anger, he continued his battle to keep visiting rights over their children. He managed to stop drinking, and though overweight now, carried on his job, and met another woman, whom he married. This isn't a head-over-heels romance, but he's far happier than he was with Sonia. He feels peaceful, though at times he still weeps when he thinks about Wendy and Barbara. Valerie helps him a lot, especially when he has time to visit his girls, and she has managed to keep a place in her nieces' affections.

This story exemplified the selfish behavior of a narcissist who formed and used a trauma bond with the man she married, and hid her agenda remarkably well until it was no longer necessary. Réne did everything for her, as he had been doing for his mother, never questioning whether Sonia wasn't the one being jealous and selfish, until it was very late. He needed to have realized that Sonia never loved him - only his attention, and the money she knew he would get from his mother's inheritance. This is why, once the mother died, she had herself an affair and flaunted it; then made a show of going and coming back. That got Réne anxious to have her back, at the time he had money again. Once that was assured, she had another affair with a "more important", probably wealthy, man, having his child to force him to marry her, once she'd divorced Réne. Quite obviously, Sonia never loved anyone in all of this heartbreaking mess, except herself. What Réne needs to do is to keep on healing and growing in himself, and to try to have the best influence he can over Wendy and Barbara.

TORMENTING, COVERT NARCISSISTS AND STOCKHOLM-SYNDROME TRAUMA BONDS

KONRAID Y. FINEBUCK

Joe Adams was one of the ten or so younger employees of the large company that manufactured control systems for conveyor-belts and industrial processes. He was quieter than average, and shy, except in situations where he felt more at home - work wasn't one of them. He struggled not so much with the technical aspects (even though he tended to over-correct himself in these), as with negotiations and social relations with their customers. An important, rather arrogant factory-manager, but not technically-qualified with regard to the conveyor-belts, could end up shouting at him, or putting him under pressure, and Joe didn't handle that very well.

Konraid Finebuck was one of his colleagues. On occasion the two of them had worked together on a project, or had been part of a team of three or four technicians. They weren't friends, but they could and did work together uneventfully. In fact, Konraid was a rather uneventful worker, most of them would have said at the company. He was tall, blond, rather quiet, but not actually shy. One might have said, as Joe did to himself, that "Kon" was somewhat cynical. Nevertheless, he was part of the office conversations and the general banter, though never the main speaker.

Joe sometimes admitted to himself that he was a bit envious of Kon. This sounds rather strange, but the fact that Kon was so much a part of the crowd, quite capable at his job when he wanted to be (Kon just coasted along; at that point he wasn't putting much effort into his work), and yet he didn't stand out or get attention, all made him seem to be in a much better position than Joe, who hated attention because for him it usually involved making fun of him, or putting some sort of expectation on him. Joe was envious of quite a lot of the others, not just

186

Kon. He didn't like the way he felt when he sensed envy, because there was hopelessness underlying it.

One day some of Joe's colleagues, all still single, were in the office talking, boasting about their romantic escapades of the weekend before. Joe was also single, and had never had a girlfriend. He never joined in such conversations: they were rather crude; he was deeply religious, and he was shy, in any case. At times they made fun of him; sometimes they did so enjoying his embarrassment, at others without realizing how sensitive he was. Then the conversation faded as they got stuck into their office-work.

"Hey, Joe! You posted a French letter last weekend, didn't ya?" said a voice right behind him, suddenly. Joe spun round in his office chair, to see Konraid staring at him with the most mocking, the most malicious, the most intense stare you ever saw. It actually made Joe Adams jump. "Oh, come on, Kon! You know I don't just sleep around."
Someone came into the office with a question, and it distracted them all. In any case, Kon had already moved off to his desk.

Joe's mind puzzled over what Kon had just done. He thought, "Kon does sometimes join in when they're ragging me. Yet I've never seen him with a weird, intense stare like that. I felt as if I'd been knifed in my back by an invisible blade." He shrugged it off. An hour later, Kon and two other colleagues went out to make a site-visit. Joe was looking at his computer-screen when someone knocked hard against his chair, shaking him. It was Konraid (Y. Finebuck!), walking past. "Did he do that deliberately?" asked Joe to himself.

The next week or so was very difficult for Joe. Kon seemed to have changed, but for no known reason. He began to greet Joe every morning, but we say, 'greet' in the sense of a smirking, short, threatening few words, just, "G'morning, Joe". Things started happening in the office. Or did they? Someone - and it couldn't have been Kon - put chewing-gum on his chair. How infantile! That day Kon was away on a project all day, and all day the day thereafter. Later in the week, Joe had a two-page report ready to print out to take to a meeting. When he looked for it at the last-minute on the computer, in the "Meetings" folder, it wasn't there! Cursing and swearing despite himself, he searched frantically, but it wasn't on the system. He had to copy a few pages of information, print them instead, and then 'fudge' for facts when he made his contribution in the meeting. Afterwards, their boss wanted to read their reports, whether printed, or electronically; Joe had to apologize that his wasn't ready, and start all over again afterwards, making up his report from scratch. The boss was slightly angry, but he believed it was a genuine loss, not a failure to do his work, because Joe had a reputation for being honest.

It could have been possible for Kon - or someone else - to have entered Joe's desktop computer. All the computers had a shared password, because they were all connected to the same company network. Yet was it really Kon? Had Joe not made some kind of a mistake, and deleted the file? (But there was no evidence of it among his deleted files. Anyway, you would have to wipe it out completely. That was possible for Kon to have done, though.) Joe had a tendency to be scatter-brained. He'd once sent an email to the wrong clients... Above all, if it was Konraid, WHY, WHY and WHY?

There was no known incident he could think of when Joe might have laughed at, left out, or otherwise offended his colleague. Other incidents happened where people made funny remarks to him, that were unusual. A mysterious letter turned up in Joe's mailbox at home. It was pasted together from cut newspaper headlines, reading, "If you don't put your car away in your garage, we are gonna slash your tires!!" He crumpled it in anger, and threw it away.

Joe's mind reeled in confusion. Perhaps these were unrelated incidents. Or maybe he was just "losing it"? He felt a weird kind of excitement in his rather boring life, coupled with a sense of shame and unworthiness. He was losing the will to find out what the truth was about what was happening... but at the same time, paradoxically, he was becoming angry. What was Kon's problem? Not only did he sense all these feelings, but Joe Adams realized that he was starting to feel not just envy, but admiration, for Kon.

188

Admiration? Yes, Kon could be seen to be master of his situation. You could hear him make a suggestion, crack a joke, say a few words... and people started to agree with him, or change the tone of their views. He could be "average", but had respect without excess responsibility. He seemed to be able to control or manipulate one or two of his colleagues who were his friends, who were both rather silly and insecure types. Why hadn't Joe seen this before? Poor Joe felt so confused by the chaos that swirled in his head, that he just wished they could send him to Timbuktu on an assignment. He wouldn't come back! (Or they could send Kon...!)

He felt as if the devil were playing with the situation at work, pulling invisible strings like a puppet-master. Why did he envy Kon, since for all that man's ability to influence, and get by in life, he wasn't a particularly kind or sympathetic character? He almost tortured himself with thinking about it, what he could have done to deserve it all, but came up with nothing.

This situation - charged with too many incidents of mockery from other people who seemed to have been influenced, petty sabotage, snide comments from Kon, and general confusion - took its toll on Joe, who couldn't sleep properly. He began to forget things more and more, and seemed to be daydreaming at times. One day in the office, Kon stopped beside Joe's desk and waved something in front of him. "Here's a rubber for you, buddy." Joe snapped inside himself, grabbing a manual and a calendar from his desk and lashing out, knocking the condom in its packet out of Kon's hand. Kon's face twisted into laughter, and their colleagues wondered why Joe was in such a bad mood. Joe had basically accepted that Konraid was trying to do something to him with subtle malice, though he didn't have a clue why.

Eventually, Joe found himself standing on a balcony at the top of a high building, feeling suicidal. He agonized over what he was considering, for he had always been taught that suicide is a sin. Yet he said to himself that life didn't seem right to live any more, that he wanted to die, at any rate just didn't want to carry on as he was. Fortunately someone saw him there, for it was a place where a couple of people had actually committed suicide, and several others had lingered there, as Joe was doing. They talked him out of it, and he broke down and sobbed, before pulling himself together. He gave the name of one of the elders from his church, who arrived and took him home. This man prayed with him and talked to him. He had received psychological training in his life, since he worked in Human Resources, and though he didn't like some of the more "New-Agey" or Freudian theories of the human being, he followed other methods he felt more at peace with.

Joe was frantic, but his elder worked with him. First of all, there was no doubt that Kon was doing something, and that he had shown ill-will. That last was the really important truth; what exactly he was doing, less so. Joe wanted to know why he'd been picked out. Why that sudden "knifed-in-your-back" feeling? What had he done? His elder knew about narcissism - and underlined it to Joe, repeated it, that IT WASN'T HIS FAULT. People such as Konraid Y. Finebuck (rearrange the letters...) are good at spotting potential victims, at seeing who has been traumatized already. Joe hadn't "done" any more than move into the sights of his abuser. Joe talked about his feelings of envy, crying and ashamed, and the strange kind of attraction he felt to Kon. Did it mean that Joe was gay? Was it just because they all had girlfriends, and he didn't?

The elder had enough sense not to blast Joe with a condemnation. Though he may very well have believed that all gay relationships are little more than a narcissist using his victim or victims (which happens also in heterosexual relationships, we add, but this hardly makes all heterosexual relationships destructive or narcissistic!), he was wise enough to know about Stockholm Syndrome!

"Joe, have you ever heard of 'Stockholm Syndrome'?" he asked. Joe hadn't. It was explained to him how, in a situation where you are vulnerable, your mind sees no way out but to try to be submissive, to please whoever has power over you. Though Joe had never got to the point of pleading for mercy, his feelings of shame were stoked up, which a narcissist has considerable skill in using. So Joe was able to understand his reaction: that broke the power it had over him. At church they prayed with him, asking for the power to stand firm in his mind, and to deal with Konrad in a spirit of calm indifference.

In the days following, Joe returned Konraid's menacing greeting each day with a pleasant but brief salutation, "Good morning, Kon." He steeled himself not to keep on looking to see where Kon was when he was in the office. When he had to go on a site visit with Kon, he was glad of having a third man there, but tried to keep calm and talk about the work. Just once, he saw Kon whisper in the ear of one of his 'minion' friends in the office, and at the end of that day a silly prank was done: a ballpoint-pen refill without the writing-end was put into the glass that held Joe's pens and pencils, so that its ink leaked out overnight. It was quite possible for Kon's minion to have been the one who slipped it in at the end of the day, for that guy had been one of the few still there when Joe left work. Joe just put the glass into a plastic bag, said calmly, "This is really infantile", and dealt with it at home.

Joe's hardest test came a few weeks later, when one of his colleagues asked him the question he'd guessed he'd have to face: "Is it true you went up on the balcony of the hotel tower?" (By implication, to throw himself off.) The news had traveled. Joe acknowledged that it was true, but that he'd been given prayer and counseling at his church; that he'd been having a bad time, but it was over then, and he was handling life better. The colleague wasn't exactly being kind and understanding, but it seemed to satisfy him. Their boss never questioned him about it. Then, two days later...

...Joe opened a drawer in his desk, to find an A4 sheet of paper with the outline figure of a man sketched on it, some lines suggesting coming down from above, and a starring pattern depicting his slamming down onto a hard surface. Jumping off a high place? For a second he felt as if he was going to explode with rage, but he reminded himself: "I'm not giving my abuser what he wants. I'm going to let God control my life, not him!" Joe Adams made as if nothing had happened. He decided not to report the incident (would it help him regarding his manager, to admit having been suicidal? Probably not.), and he got on with his job.

Evidently Konraid hadn't changed his attitude; but Joe knew he had changed his own. Joe wasn't giving his abuser the kind of "narcissistic supply" that Kon wanted, so he'd been left alone much more. After this last attempt, Kon seemed to have given up trying to torment Joe. A few months later, Joe got another job. It wasn't "paradise after hell", but it was better; and not just because Kon wasn't a part of it! Konraid actually began to put a lot more effort into his work, and was promoted to a more senior position in the firm, but in another city. Soon after, he got a very well-paid job there, with another company. Yet Joe doesn't envy him; Joe has learned how to be stronger in himself. He's going out with a girl who likes him and, just as importantly, respects him.

Is there another victim in Konraid Y. Finebuck's life, now? Everything explained about trauma and abusers suggests that there will be more of them, as there were probably a few before Joe Adams. Just exactly how much damage will "Kon" do in his life? He has a taste for hidden power; Joe never tried to get him into trouble, working out in his quiet way that Konraid would retaliate viciously. What about the rest of them? Some of them noticed that Kon "teased" Joe, but since some of them were doing so as well, they never saw the malice in his efforts. Many never saw a thing! We believe that some 'Narcs' can be very dangerous precisely because they get away with a lot, unseen - and yet they have a strong ability to influence many people around them. How will it all end? When Konraid is fifty years old, will his business partner, tormented, used, confused, and "sucked dry" of his money, turn up at Kon's office and shoot him dead, before turning the gun on himself?

Whatever may happen, Joe's actions show how a victim of Stockholm Syndrome, a type of trauma-bond in less intimate or personal situations, can take back control of his or her life. Joe asked for help; he came to understand that he was picked out simply in order to be abused; that he wasn't to feel shame or guilt for how he felt; that he had to be strong and calm within himself, and not try to retaliate. Joe can say that he's forgiven Konraid, and moved on, without in any way excusing what was done to him. He can see that such immature and infantile tricks are a poor reflection of Kon's character, but that they should be treated with indifference. The only tragedy is that Kon got away with it, as 'Narcs' seem to do (or for a time! More on that in the last chapter...), but Joe is a stronger man because of what he learned about healing himself of his childhood and teenage wounds, and the abuse that took advantage of them.

VERA VENOMA

Vera Venoma is a junior school teacher. She has her registry class, that is to say, where they all report who is present at the beginning of the day. She is the teacher who writes their school reviews and reports from the information given by the teachers of different subjects. All the kids fear her...

Every little boy and girl comes to know that you don't want to fall victim to Miss Venoma; because every year she chooses a victim. Maybe he's a boy who doesn't tie his shoelaces and writes the letter 'B' backwards-way-round; maybe she's a girl who lisps and can't remember her seven-times table. Just possibly, it's the boy who can't sit still, and tries to pull the girls' hair tied into pigtails when the teacher has her back turned. May God help that victim...

She uses sarcasm and shame. If the victim's book isn't neatly-written, if she's made grammar-mistakes or written a date wrongly... the book will be shown to the class.
"This... MESS... is Joanna's history homework. I read: 'Critsofer Columbus discovered the americas in 1941.' First of all: nineteen forty-one is seventy-nine years ago. Maybe your grandparents were born then. Does anybody have a grandfather or grandmother who's seventy-nine years old, or even older? You do, Jeannie? How old? Eighty-one? Your 'grandpa'. Good girl. So... when your grandfather was born, America hadn't even been discovered! Oh? Your 'grandpa' was born in Sacramento? That's in the USA... isn't it, Joanna?" A snide glare is turned to Joanna, who's been looking at the floor. She says nothing.

"So, let's get this straight. What you were SUPPOSED to write, to copy off the board, was the year FOURTEEN NINETY-ONE. That's FIVE

HUNDRED, TWENTY-NINE years ago! Joanna doesn't know the difference between five hundred, twenty-nine years, and seventy-nine years!" By this time, Joanna is crying quietly. "That means, if you sent "Genius" Joanna to the supermarket to buy seventy-nine dollars of groceries, she'd happily take out five hundred, thirty dollars, and expect to get ONE dollar back!" Muffled laughter spreads through the class. Mirth mixed with fear!

"Secondly: Joanna has written 'CRITSOFER', that is, 'critt-so-furr'." Vera pronounces the misspelling with a snarl. "What is wrong with that, anybody? Apart from the fact that it sounds like 'sofa'! Yes, Manuel?"
"It's C H R I S T O P H E R, Ma'am."
"That's right. I put it up on the board. It's written in your history textbook. But it seems Joanna was someplace else, so she didn't know. Maybe in Boston? Or China?" Joanna is crying louder. "Now, what is this word, 'americas'? Who can tell me what's wrong with what she wrote? Jeannie? Yes, it needs a CAPITAL letter. Just like your name, because it's a proper NAME. Or does Joanna spell her name with a small letter at the beginning?" More muffled laughter. "Or maybe a 'w'? 'Jo-wannah'?"

Crushed Joanna cries on quietly. Vera slams the exercise book down, and says: "When I give you homework, you make sure it's done properly. If you don't remember how it's spelled, LOOK IN YOUR HISTORY BOOK, AND YOU'LL SEE HOW!!"

Really, there are very few discipline problems in Vera Venoma's class. Outside, the victims churn in fear when they're on their way to History, as do quite a lot of the class, as well. Hardly anyone likes History...

This situation comes to the ears of June and Gerry, the parents of little Justin. Their son is talking away happily about what he'd done that day at school, and he gets onto the topic of the History class and his teacher, also his registry teacher. They are horrified. Their son has just taken it all at face value, as children do so often. It seems that this happens every year. Justin is scared of Miss Venoma, but he does quite well at History, and therefore he reasons that he'll be OK. June and Gerry realize that little Joanna is dyslexic, and cannot help herself. She needs training in reading, rather than getting mockery. The parents hear more about Miss Venoma from other parents, and decide to see the head teacher.

The head, the school principal, is one of the calm, "hands-off" types who stays in his office and looks at the examination results, and checks other figures of his pupils' social background, presumed household income and home language. On paper, the school is doing well. So when June and Gerry come to see him, he cannot understand why they are bothered: "But you're telling me that Justin's doing well?"
"Yes, HE is. But we're hearing all about Miss Venoma's tactics, and, quite frankly, we're shocked."
"I hear what you're saying. All our pupils are important at Sand Hills School. But I've never personally had any complaints against Miss Venoma, and I can't call her out over what some of the kids say about her. They don't always understand why you have to put in an effort and do your best, you know! Do you realize the History marks went up an average of ten percent since she started?" Quite obviously, that day Justin's parents aren't going to get anywhere with the principal.

In class, Vera has an ally. She's called Jeannie - yes, you heard her name already. Jeannie was terrified of Miss Venoma at first, but she tried her best in History. One day she was called to stay back after class. Vera looked at Jeannie in a way that showed she was summing her up; and asked her if she knew about who broke the window at the back of the Sports Hall, and whether it was true that Joanna's mother was drunk at home in the afternoon... Jeannie did her best to fill Vera in on the latest gossip.

Vera made a promise to Jeannie: "If you tell me what I want to know, and you do your best in my class, I'll put your name forward when the Principal wants to know who the prefects should be for next year." Ever since then, Jeannie does her best in History, and tells Vera about any tale she hears. Jeannie comes from a home where her parents argue, and she gets very little love and attention, especially not from her mother. This information is given to her teachers through the schools' psychologist, and other, informal channels. Soon, Jeannie begins to admire her History teacher, and to see a substitute-mother in Vera; even though she's a hard task-mistress.

The Principal does have a word privately with Vera. Vera Venoma is so surprised: she looks innocent and quietly hurt. The mother and father of little Justin? "I've never had any problems with him. Yes, I always insist that everybody does their best, and I point out mistakes so no-one gets their facts wrong. I mean, they're mostly doing well." It sounds quite satisfactory.

The news also comes to Vera through her protegé. Justin tells some of his friends that his Mom and Dad said Miss Venoma was unkind, and that he shouldn't make fun of Joanna even if the other kids do. Words spread like runaway fires, and Jeannie hears about what Justin's parents said. She tells Vera excitedly. Vera seems cool and unconcerned: "Jeannie, you know that if you do what I say, everything's all right in my class, hey, honey? So don't worry about me."

It isn't long before Vera hits back. She tells her minion Jeannie to find out anything she can about Justin, because "Justin seems to be behaving badly, but his Mom and Dad don't want to hear about it." A week or so later, Jeannie comes triumphantly to her mentor, to tell Vera that she's heard Justin and a couple of his friends have been smoking cigarettes in the afternoon, behind the Sports Hall. Vera seizes this news with glee: she instructs Jeannie to go near there and watch from a distance; and if the boys are there and they're smoking, then she has to go straight to the school Principal and report them. This is exactly what happens. June and her husband Gerry are ashamed of their son's behavior when they're told, but they have a nasty feeling that this has something to do with their earlier complaint to the school, and Justin seems to agree with that. However, Justin's told by his parents that HE'D better behave, and then there won't be any reason to fear Miss Venoma!

Vera carries on making Joanna's life a misery. When her History textbook gets a red stain on one of the pages, Vera sees and Joanna is questioned: "What is that?"

"It was fruit juice, Ma'am." Joanna can hardly whisper, and she's shaking.

"FRUIT JUICE?! Look at this! Look, everybody!" Vera holds up the offending textbook. "Do you know that every textbook costs over thirty dollars? And she spills fruit juice on it! Or is it fruit juice? Maybe it's wine..."

Joanna is staring hard at the floor. "No."

"I don't know whether to believe you. And the question is, if it's wine, were you drinking it, or was it your MOTHER?!" Some children laugh...

This is the way Vera has been managing her classes for quite a few years. However, things turn ugly. On her own initiative, without telling Vera, Jeannie sends an anonymous message on social media to some of the girls at the school: it says, "Guess whose school clothes smell of booze?" All the girls who get it know who it refers to, some send it on, and a few of them start teasing Joanna about the insinuation. Another message appears: "Jowanna! Your Mommy's jwunk again." That is the last straw for their victim.

A few days later, Joanna isn't at school. She's in hospital, having overdosed on whiskey and her mother's medicine. A social worker comes to talk to her, because they know that she's the child of a single mother who's an alcoholic. Joanna, rather sick, but able to speak, opens up and pours out a tale of misery, pointing to Vera Venoma.

On the side, Vera contacts Jeannie in a panic: she asks her what she knows about the anonymous messages on social media, only to have little Jeannie admit to doing it all, with joy! Jeannie is startled when Vera flies into a rage, and blames her for getting them both into trouble, for soon enough the Principal and school authorities question them. Vera puts on a flood of tears, and denies any knowledge of the offending text messages, avoiding giving any information or confession regarding her alleged comments about wine-stains on Joanna's History book, or her mistreatment of her in class.

Jeannie is very confused, frightened, and angry. So when she is questioned, she decides to tell the Principal, and the other teacher who is assisting him, the whole truth. She admits that sending the texts was her idea, but she also drops a bomb, so to speak... She tells them that she wanted to become a prefect, and to make Miss Venoma happy - and did so in return for spying on the other children, and "letting Miss Venoma touch me and kiss me."

With the social worker's gentle questioning as well, the horrified Principal and his assistant find out that lonely, unloved Jeannie has been fondled, touched between the legs and kissed by Vera, who said that she would "love her better than your Mommy does", and who had told her never to speak about it to anyone else.

This incident ends with Vera Venoma being fired from her post, and sent for what will be a very unpleasant trial, in which she will blame everyone else, and make ugly accusations: for example that Jeannie is being abused by her parents, and that is why she knows all about sexual abuse; that Jeannie is hitting back at Vera by accusing her, because Vera was angry when she was told about the sending of the offending text messages. Vera calls June and Gerry a couple of irresponsible hippies who can't control their son, and Joanna the daughter of a "white trash" alcoholic mother! As for the children: Joanna needs a lot of love, some counseling to help her to heal, and she gets remedial reading lessons. Jeannie also gets extensive trauma-counseling and after-abuse treatment, and now she's hated by all the boys and girls, and many parents as well. She ends up going to another school.

June and Gerry feel relieved that Vera Venoma is gone, but frustrated because the Principal might have apologized for not listening to them, for even though no-one knew quite how bad Vera was, it was no secret that she tormented children; but he seems to have forgotten.

In this tale of woe we can see an abuser who has two faces: one is clearly that of an abuser, the other cunningly hidden. The children see Vera for what she is, but why is it that so often, we adults don't? It is true that you have to discipline children, and that a clever, lazy one can be shamed in some circumstances. Yet, do you pick on the weak and the shy? Vera is a narcissist for whom every child is a tool to satisfy her need for power. She has the typical adeptness in finding suitable, vulnerable victims, and manages to train one of them to be an abuser, even while she is busy abusing her!

Thankfully, given the circumstances, Jeannie exposes her abuser, because she is also a victim, and a sexually-abused one at that. Many in her position would not dare to speak up. We can see the formation of a trauma-bond beginning in her, because Jeannie has begun to admire Vera deeply, even though she tells the social worker how bad she feels when Vera touches her and fondles her inappropriately. Jeannie needs to overcome that bond with Vera if she is to be a healed adult.

This cautionary tale is not meant to allege that all abusive, manipulative narcissists, whether they be teachers or not, are actual paedophiles, when it is a case of children's being badly treated. That isn't always the case. However, this is the place to say that surely, the typical sexual abuser of children is a narcissist, who feels nothing and cares nothing for anyone else, except himself or herself? How else could anyone dare to do such a thing to children? This also has relevance to the question of "rehabilitating" a convicted offender against children. We suggest that a narcissist does not change his or her attitudes, or demonstrate true remorse. It may happen that the 'Narc' modifies his or her behavior, out of necessity, but this is no guarantee that children will ever be safe with that person. Therefore we believe that an offending teacher, minister of religion, social worker, summer-camp worker, scout-leader, or whoever, should not carry on in that position, nor should an abusing parent have custody over children.

Conclusion

This book has dealt with two related topics: trauma-bonding; and the context in which it happens, toxic, abusive relationships of various kinds.

This was quite some subject to cover - the greatest of all human evils on the small-scale! Narcissistic, sociopathic attacks on, and corrupting of, love-relationships, family ties, small business interactions, friendship; exploitation of any one-to-one, or small contact in those fundamental groups out of which our society is made. And a tragic, twisted kind of love and devotion with which many of the victims imprison themselves, and are kept from being able to escape the damage already done, even allowing themselves to be traumatized further; all for someone who feels no love at all!!

Some victims are so demoralized, passive and confused that they can feel no anger, after a long time of abuse. However, those who love them, and all the recovering victims who begin to understand what happened, to accept that it wasn't their fault, who see how they were confused and used, and how much damage has been done... begin to feel great anger, and to sense injustice.

It's only human. What selfish, callous, greedy, envious, power-hungry, lustful, cold-hearted, cowardly, lying, vindictive people you hear and read about, when dealing with or describing 'Narcs'!! How little they are understood by so many of those who need to know about them, whose job it is to protect the young and the traumatized of any age. How much 'Narcs' manage to get away with, and how blind people can be to what they do! The bitterness such anger fosters inside anyone who has witnessed abuse, or who knows a victim, can cause that bystander to despair...

"How can the courts allow this? What is wrong with our prisons? Is the government asleep regarding this? Why doesn't more of the public care?" We fly into a rage thinking about it; we go further and start questioning life itself. "Why does this useless tragedy have to happen? Is the universe blind and meaningless? If there is a God, does He just turn a blind eye? Doesn't He care?"

It's a hard, hard, very deep question to reply to, and we don't pretend to have all the answers. Yet there are some things we can say from the heart, to give hope, that all is not lost...

ABUSERS DON'T JUST GET AWAY WITH IT. No! Even before they die... Remember how we said that narcissists are cold and dead inside, how they feed off the life and the attention of their victims, how they rejoice to give them pain, because doing so kills their emptiness inside? It's true! When someone decides that it's a bad world and that love isn't worth giving, chooses to live for himself or herself alone, and to seek to get as much power and pleasure out of it as possible, there is despair inside. Yes, some of them may indeed get a lot of power and pleasure in the short-term, especially when they are young. They use their looks and their health, take advantage of their talents and intelligence; and, choosing to live without the worries and self-doubt of the normal human being, seem to succeed. Their ability to influence is frightening and infuriating...

But power and pleasure last only so long! Assuming you can get them all the time... how quickly we just grow used to ANY situation. Why were readers reminded, as we remind ourselves, to cultivate thankfulness for what we have? How many of us have a home and food and drink... and other people to love, and yet take this for granted? The 'Narc', once he or she gets money, sex and a desired lifestyle, has to keep on looking for more. Why? Because they've already had them! Frantically trying to get more, as well as to keep those things they got out of the world, they start to lose pleasure, even early on in their tragic trajectory of life.

What does an egoistic maniac do, when pleasure slips away sometimes? He or she becomes bitter and angry; feeling a monstrous entitlement, they are driven to take happiness, money, love, property, and life itself from other people deemed "unworthy" of them. This sadistic, "carrion comfort" allows them to rejoice as they knowingly do harm to their victims. Deep down, it leaves them even more bitter.

What then? The greatest desire is for power. Power to change, to force other people to give them not only the things they wanted to enjoy, but just attention. The power to punish, to make people afraid of them. All of this is the theater of their deluded self-play, written inside the world they make in their heads, and which they try to wrench the real world, out there, into the shape of.

Malignant sociopaths have to fight and strive. Sometimes they succeed in attaining their objectives, to our disgust, but in this world they also fail. Circumstances cause their plans to fall through. Other people see what they want, and stop them. Some victims get away... (we hope you did, dear survivor!) Other potential victims discern what might happen to them, and stay away. Other malignant sociopaths clash with these narcissists, win, and take over. With each failure they become more and more frustrated.

A successful plot, to deceive or get control, causes a narcissist to become lazy. The law, evaded perhaps before, maybe several times, catches up with them. People who believed them, defended them, helped them, start to see the ugly truth about them, and depart in horror - sometimes in shamed silence; at other times with public denunciations and accusations!

And all of them, even the lesser ones who tyrannized just one home, family, or firm, grow old. They lose their good looks that charmed and fooled innocent people; their strife and excesses take their toll, and they look burned-out, burned out just like their addicted victims, for they are the same chemicals wreaking havoc in their brains and bodies, as in the brains and bodies of the ones they abuse. Narcissists have a considerable likelihood of becoming addicted to drugs or alcohol, also. Their vast pride and arrogance make the honest acceptance and humiliating admission of being out of control, that you have to make when you decide to stop drinking, etcetera, impossible. You, the former victim of an abuser, had to make that hard step of admitting you were bound by a false obsession that looked like love. You had to admit that you were addicted to someone who gave you pain. Imagine how hard it would be for an abuser who got power and pleasure out of life, to admit that the power and pleasure they are addicted to, have started to control them! The bitterness that comes to 'Narcs' from believing they are always right, that other people don't deserve the things they have, makes their faces look bitter.

There is an expression, "a collapsed narcissist" used to describe a 'Narc' who is aging, or is an addict, or who is beginning to grow mentally unstable. When money, power and sex are gone, the abuser can get only pity from others, or pleasure from insulting and hating them. Attention... any kind of attention. That's all that's left.

Can't you see? THIS IS A NARC. GETTING HIS OR HER OWN REWARD! Before death! Indeed, it can be said that narcissists die before they die. Perhaps an old-age home hides some of them, bitterly complaining about everything, battling the weakness and sickness we all have to face as life comes near to its end. Perhaps they hallucinate and rave in their selfish worlds. Whereas some other residents, weak and frail, wait patiently for the end; radiant with inner peace and able to be thankful for the life they had, and still have, because they still have love inside. A 'Narc' has a great big hole inside. A black hole...

What if the abuser dies young? Well, quite a few commit suicide long before they reach any great age. That suicide is a reaction of despair and emptiness, when their power over circumstances disappears, as can happen at any time, not just old age. Sometimes it is an act of revenge on those who are trauma-bonded to them. At other times it is vainglory, an attempt to look glorious and noble for a few moments before their inner hopelessness is exposed for the world to see. At other times again, it is just sheer childish sulking, that life didn't go as they wanted it to! It's all misery.

They die, all of them. What happens afterwards? Actually, given what we just said, if death really is the end of all things, then narcissists are going to lose everything they craved for. Most of them are losing it

BEFORE THEY DIE. And, if death isn't the end... then there's a hell reserved for them.

Does that make your sense of injustice feel better? Well, maybe a little. Yet the most precious truth of all is not about the 'Narc', it's about YOU!

"TO LIVE WELL IS THE BEST FORM OF REVENGE!"

We put this to you: if at this very moment, a great bolt of lightning could strike that abuser who's been wrecking your life, and turn him or her into a small, black pile of ashes... Would that solve all your problems?

OK, it would stop the outward abuse! Yet you get that result if you can leave your abuser and have no contact. The fact is, that you are left walking wounded, your happiness and peace robbed from you, and the despair which rotted away inside your abuser threatening to get inside you. You are left with a crazy feeling of love for them, even when you know that you didn't and couldn't love what they were. That's what it was like to be a trauma-bonded victim.

The saying quoted above, introduced to English by George Herbert, and probably of Iberian origin (Spanish, Portuguese, or the Talmud), is worth a thousand fine words about how to get over a trauma bond! This is better than any form of revenge.

Dear victim, you are ALIVE! You are looking to the future, and you have hope. Yours is the golden opportunity to make the most of what you have. Yours, the opportunity to love. To love yourself, in the healthiest way, to heal yourself so that you can start loving other people the way they really are. Not the cardboard characters you looked for desperately in your trauma; but the people who will, or already do, really love you.

You need to break free, so that what your narcissist does or doesn't do is no longer of any interest or relevance to you. You will have forgiven them. That isn't, excused. It's a decision of the will, not the feelings, to acknowledge they did wrong, let them go, and not to seek revenge. To decide to be free of them. Because you have far better and worthier things to do with your time and life.

We described what happened to you in trauma, probably in your childhood, and any other extreme crises in your life. We described how later on, in an adult love-relationship, or what should be love and pleasure, the relationship becomes a trap where old hurts and pains are re-lived for the selfish needs of a sociopathic 'Narc' who has decided to get everything he or she can, out of you, and who feels no love for you or anyone else, except himself or herself (and doesn't do even that very well!)

This was to help you to open your eyes and see what was going on; you were shown how it wasn't your fault, and why it is so hard to understand your reactions.

Some techniques, and understanding of your emotions, were explained to you, so that you could learn how to control your feelings, and how to think clearly. We mentioned how to look after and be kind to your body, as the body is deeply involved in your recovery from trauma and addiction.

Some questions and answers, and some examples, have been given to you to steer you through recovery. Over and over again, we urged you to open up to caring and knowledgeable people, to therapists, support-groups and other trusted figures in your life. Life is not a battle to fight alone (wasn't that what putting up with your abuser ended in being?); but it is a fight, though! We made it clear that there are some things inside you, that you and you alone need to do, to achieve freedom. You'll feel so much better when you've done them! It's worth it all!

Love, that over-used word, is what it's all about. It really isn't a second-hand emotion, once there's nothing 'narcky' about its object, and nothing traumatized about you, any more. Love is quite prepared to suffer, but only for the truth, rather than a desperate illusion. Like a marathon, if you run it, there is a prize; even better than a marathon, the prize starts to come to you along the way!

Made in the USA
Las Vegas, NV
20 October 2023

79392504R00115